THE SHADOWS BENEATH THE PEWS

THE ASSAULT AGAINST THE CHURCH BY THE SPIRIT OF ADDICTION

Dr. EURAL ALEXANDER

MARVELOUS LIGHT PUBLICATIONS • WEST BLOOMFIELD, MICHIGAN

The Shadows Beneath the Pews:
The Assault Against the Church by the Spirit of Addiction

Copyright © 2017 by Rev. Dr. Eural Alexander

All rights reserved.
Published by Marvelous Light Publications.

Amplified,1987, Zondervan Publishing, Grand Rapids, MI
ESV, 2001 Crossway Bibles, Wheaton, IL
King James Version, 1988, Liberty University Press, Lynchburg, VA
MSG, 2002, NavPress, Colorado Springs, CO
NASB, 1995, Lockman Foundation, LaHabra, CA
NIV, 2000, Zondervan, Grand Rapids, MI
NCV, 1991, Thomas Nelson Publishers, Nashville, TN
NLT, 2016, Tyndale House, Carol Stream, IL

No part of this publication may be stored in a retrieval system, transmitted in any form or reproduced by any means: electronic, mechanical, photocopying, recording, or otherwise without written permission from the publisher, author, and illustrators.

ISBN: 978-0-9774662-2-1

Cover and Interior Design & Layout
LaTanya Orr • www.iselah.com

Printed in The United States of America

PRAISE FOR "THE SHADOWS BENEATH THE PEWS"

"*The Shadows Beneath the Pews,* is a crystal clear, written illustration of spiritual addiction problems within the Church. Dr. Alexander gives answers to the problems and how the Church, with God's unmatchable power, is capable of ditching her mask of denial, thus, overcoming its spirit of addiction."

    Sterling H. Brewer
    District Moderator, New Rising Star of Hope
    Senior Pastor, King David Missionary Baptist Church

"A must read! *The Shadows Beneath the Pews-The Assault Against the Church by the Spirit of Addiction* is a book that echoes God's original intent of totally depending on God to fight the spirit of addiction in the Church. Dr. Alexander challenges us to see the power of addiction and to also discover and claim the power of God over it. He has provided tools of survival to overcome the assault of addiction by allowing God to order your steps and your mind to be victorious when such a deep struggle threatens your life and spiritual growth. By reading this amazing book, you are challenged to recognize that when you are threatened by a spirit that seeks to take God's place within you, then you fight for your external growth and life in the Lord."

    Rev. Dr. Deedee M. Coleman
    President, Council of Baptist Pastors of Detroit & Vicinity, Inc., Detroit, MI; Pastor, Russell Street Baptist Church

"Dr. Alexander's powerful and profound book truly bespeaks the anointing that God has divinely invested in his life to spiritually combat this social ill within the church and our wider community. In fact, you can literally hear this man of God's heart on every page because he wholeheartedly wants God's people who are bound by various addictions, to experience the power of God that's at work in their lives once they acknowledge their weaknesses and afterwards seek His face. Through his own experiences, Dr. Alexander gives us insight into how we can effectively meet people at their needs so that they can subsequently make decisions that will bring about a deliverance in their life. I highly recommend that you add this book to your library so that God's people can live more abundantly and experience spiritual wholeness. In a word, this book is impactful!"

    Rev. Jim Holley, Ph.D.
    Senior Pastor, Historic Little Rock Baptist Church

"A powerful and thought provoking work. While the book's major theme is addiction and the church, Dr. Alexander also explores the relationship between the community at large and the church. He takes the reader on a journey to observe the impact of addiction on the church and the broader community. As a Pastor, teacher and counselor, he points out the importance of acknowledging and addressing the spirit of addiction whenever and wherever it shows up. "

Shirley R. Stancato, LL.D.
President & CEO, New Detroit, Inc.

"Dr. Eural Alexander, whose well trained and highly experienced career in clinical counseling and personal ministry, offers us a glimpse into the precarious paradigm of the pathology of the pew and the predicament of the pulpit as we attack the spirit of addiction in the church. The church is not a museum for saints, but a hospital for sinners. Dr. Alexander unearths the warfare in a battle that the church must win. This comprehensive treatise deals with this urgent issue both systematically and spiritually. Dr. Eural Alexander is a blessing to the Body of Christ."

Bishop Edgar L. Vann II
Senior Pastor, Second Ebenezer Church

"Dr. Eural Alexander has shed light on a subject that may seem taboo in the church realm. He has taken his experiences, both past and present, and merged them to give us a personal, professional and spiritual introspective view into the world of addiction and its overshadowing, yet silent assault on the church. His passion to help those chained by addiction radiates in every chapter as he helps us understand the suffering of an addict and his pleas to the church to no longer ignore this binding spirit and prepare for Spiritual warfare. *The Shadows Beneath the Pews* is a must read for clergy struggling with how to recognize and handle the spirit of addiction within their congregation and/ or community."

Darlene L. Womack
Human Resources Professional

DEDICATION

To my Parents, the late John and Sallie Alexander, who loved me, never gave up on me and knew that I belonged to God even when the addicting spirits thought I belonged to them.

*To my wife, Dr. Beverly Alexander, who loves me, supports my dreams and always sees the God in me, the best in me; and to those who have made the decision after reading this book to walk a new life path, one of freedom from addiction's bondage.
May God richly bless you.*

ACKNOWLEDGEMENTS

Thank you Mother and Father, for your endless nights of prayer and your unwavering love and concern for me while I struggled to grow-up and become the man in which God purposed me to be. I know you are loving heaven!

Thank you Darlene and Jeffrey Womack, for reigniting the fire within me to complete my God-given mandate to pen this work.

Thank you to the award-winning LaTanya Orr, for your patience, assistance and expertise in developing this project.

Thanks to the members of God's church of which I am the humble under-Shepherd, New Light Family Christian Center, for your exhortations, supplications, prayers and intercessions as I pressed to finish this book.

Thanks to my amazing wife, Beverly, for your countless hours of prayers, editing and consulting on this project. I am blessed by God to have such an anointed woman of God laboring alongside me who is my wife, soulmate, best friend, companion, and co-pastor.

Thank You Beautiful Triune God, my First Love, Strong Tower, Rock, Redeemer, Deliverer, Conqueror, Friend, Soon Coming King and so much more as there is not enough space to inscribe Your diverse attributes for which I intimately know You- thank You for trusting me with Kingdom assignments over and over, for equipping me with everything needed to get the job done and for being right next to me through it all. Nothing or no one can compare to You.

TABLE OF CONTENTS

FOREWORD   i

INTRODUCTION   vii

CHAPTER ONE
THE SECRET IS OUT: THE DEVIL IS A LIAR   1

CHAPTER 2 - A COMMUNITY UNDER SIEGE   19

CHAPTER 3 - WE WERE CREATED IN
THE IMAGE OF GREATNESS   49

CHAPTER 4 - YOU ARE NOT ALONE   71

CHAPTER 5 - THERE IS NO PLACE LIKE HOME   87

_____

ABOUT THE AUTHOR

FOREWORD

God chooses whom He pleases to uncover compulsions in His church. If we are not addicted to God, if God is not our prime compulsion, then more than likely, whatever is our addiction is in need of God's deliverance.

God is jealous. Whatever replaces God as our foremost priority, whatever separates us from Him, whatever distracts us from being the kings and queens that He created us - with purpose - to be, quite frankly, angers Him. Such is the cyclical epidemic of substance abuse.

Substance abuse is a distraction designed to strip one's authority, cloud one's judgment, and separate one from God. The enslavement of God's people by means of diverse substances displeases God, even makes Him angry. After all, substance control over any life is the enemy's declaration of war against God's creation. So then "using" is a spiritual assault that attacks and takes over one's mental faculties so that one's physical body may ultimately be destroyed.

Using begins as a clandestine relationship. It prefers a closeted romance. There, no one can witness the havoc and utter destruction using wreaks on the life it has intimately targeted to destroy, especially when Christians are the victims.

My husband, Eural Alexander, is a bold and courageous Kingdom warrior, who doesn't fear potential consequences for exposing "secrets" that make their way into the sanctuary. Secrets in the church tend to slip in, slip away, and hide beneath the pews. That way, just like a closet with a closed door, secrets can't be seen, can't be heard and are undiscoverable until someone opens the door. Shhhhhhh!

God is using Eural in these last days to help free and help heal an enslaved people bound by the enemy through substance abuse's clutches. His gift of discernment coupled with his personal experiences of having danced with the dark one, blesses Eural to feel the captive's pain, spot addiction's grasp, call it out in the name of Jesus, and witness God's delivering grace. He has shared with me many personal, soul gripping stories from the canvas of his past. The pictures that once hung in his personal gallery of destruction and death caused many to cast him off as a casualty of war. But God had different plans for Eural, as evidenced in this, his first published work.

Having received his ministerial call at a tender age, the enemy quickly ensnared my husband and he began using. Too much use morphed into abuse. Yet, despite this dependency on substances, Eural still pressed his way to church. The strong tug from heaven on his heart couldn't keep him away. You see, his mother and strong woman of faith, Sallie Pearl Alexander, reared him in the fear and admonition of the Lord. She knew who he was and nurtured his future position by training him in the way that he should go. When the efficacy of addiction triggered resistance to Eural's calling, Sallie Pearl prayed for her baby boy. Especially then, miraculously, he made his way to the sanctuary.

His then pastor loved Eural dearly and rebuked any member who attempted to deny him access to the sanctuary. His pastor recognized the call and anointing on Eural's life and was certain that if Eural continued to stagger his way to assemble with the saints in the presence of God, deliverance would be his ultimate gift. The church, in this pastor's eyes, had a plethora of obligations to the community, one of which was to allow the wounded access to God's transformative power.

The church is indeed a hospital for the spiritually sick. If an addicted soul, however, wobbles his or her way into God's hospital and is turned away at the door because of their obvious altered state, then the church, - the elect body of believers, - has not performed the spiritual triage necessary to rid the addicted saints of that which plagues. Then the church, - the elect anointed men and women of God, - has not stood in the gap praying with intent and expectation, so that the spirit which plagues those addicted souls is rebuked, loosed and defeated in the presence of God. There is an expectation that if one can just make it to the sanctuary, - freedom, deliverance can happen!

The Shadow Beneath the Pews speaks to those users who press their way to the sanctuary hoping that Jesus will meet him or her there, just as He met the woman at the well. He met the woman right where she was – physically, spiritually, emotionally and psychologically. He peered into her soul, disclosed her past, exposed her present and proposed her a future. Jesus's proposal to the woman was freedom from an addiction of existence devoid of His grace, via a fount possessing an endless reservoir of access to His grace as well as access to His power, His love, His mercy and His eternal presence.

I believe that Eural's first body of work is for every secret user hiding in the pew, hoping to be found by Jesus. If you are struggling with drug dependency and this book finds its way into your hands, I pray that through these words, you will be inspired to admit your helplessness as a prisoner of addiction and cry out to God. More so and effectually, I pray that through the words on the following pages, when you cry out, God will hear you and show you great and mighty things you can never imagine. Praying still, as you embrace this work, that Jesus the Liberator will show up and patch up all your leaks, mend your brokenness, heal your every wound and deliver you from the bondage of addiction. And, that when you meet Jesus in the beauty of holiness, you will smile and tell Him "yes" and "thank you." Then, as these inscriptions take root in your heart, my final prayer for you, O courageous one, is that you will intently, live the purposeful life of greatness for which you were fashioned by God's own hands. Read on!

- Beverly Alexander, D.Min.

INTRODUCTION

As a child growing up and attending church services with my family, I recall the church being a place of refuge from the outside world. The sanctuary of our church always had a welcoming atmosphere. Upon entering the room the problematic social issues, which were impacting our lives outside the solace of the church, seemed to go away. However, social matters that were once kept securely outside the confines of the church walls had now positioned themselves inside the church in a most visibly frightening manner.

When asked in congregations across our nation if there were any concerns regarding the possibility of church members being substance abusers, many church attendees found it hard to believe. Most refused to accept that addiction or substance abuse has found its way into the pews of America's churches. The very thought of members being addicted to any agent saddens the hearts of many devoted Christians.

Addiction, however, seems apparent when we take a closer examination of the compulsive and obsessive lifestyles of many believers in our churches today. Once a taboo social behavior in the community, we now find that the social acceptance of addiction has indeed surfaced in many churches across our nation in unbelievable numbers. It could be said that believers have enough to deal with outside the walls of the church, but we must begin to protect the institution of the house of God more so now, than any other time in the history of the New Testament church.

I believe that addictions of any kind begin with a demonic influence, which is introduced to the mindset of the user. Because of the demonic forces which are warehoused in addiction, nonbelievers are continually enticed to participate in chronic addictive behaviors, and because they lack spiritual direction, use substances over and over again with no spiritual support of which to turn. This, however, should not be the case with Christians; but amazingly, the influences of addiction have managed to forcefully entice believers as well into its web. Sadly, both groups are certain to hit bottom because of the continued influences of imps on their minds.

The desire to use substances begins in the user's mind. Once the thought is entertained, addiction begins a process which I call the "spiritual relapse syndrome." These continued relapse occurrences encourage the user to engage in pathological substance abuse in spite of the adverse consequences before them. As for believers, continued pathological use motivates a return to old lifestyles of club hopping, drinking, smoking, and secular living. These actions are blinded by a lack of understanding that this shift in behavior is simply a trap set by Satan.

Initially, when I first began to write this book, I too was taken aback on how and when the infiltration of addiction in the church began. But I now understand that the recent infiltration of addiction in the faith community is also an organized plan initiated by Satan.

As a result of my learnings over the years, I felt a call by God to educate, and to bring additional insight to the church and the community relative to the mental, emotional, and physical dynamics developed in the wake of addiction.

The Father has led me to discuss how parishioners' addiction elicited issues of brokenness within the congregation. He has charged me to bring a new awareness to the church on the use of substances by members of the body of Christ. What every believer must accept is that addiction to any agent stagnates believers' spiritual growth and it ultimately presents problems in the church, specifically in the area of the church's spiritual growth. Finally, there is a need to disclose and illuminate the impact chemical dependency has on the surrounding communities of the houses of worship, both culturally and socially.

When not addressed, this particular satanic spirit, which best describes addiction, promotes a deception that the church has a permissible attitude toward the use of substances in and around the community, as well as within the church's congregations. While this is so far from the truth, unfortunately, the social decay resulting from mass incidents of addiction has forced many religious entities to close its doors. Many houses of worship have had to pack up their belongings and abandon their mission due to the destructive impact substance addiction has had on the membership, the ministry and the community.

Congregations across America have fought hard to grow and establish their presence in urban communities. However, because of Satan's relentless attacks, congregations have had to say goodbye to the hopes and dreams of their ministry, unable to overcome the onslaught of demonic attacks. This pattern of defeatism is becoming the norm for too many congregations. Because of the all-consuming power of the "spirit of addiction" affecting the people of God and neighboring communities, many believe all hope is lost. How unfortunate!

It is perplexing that in our society today, many believers and nonbelievers alike are well aware of the devastating blow substances can cause, yet still believe they are "different" and will not succumb to its affects. Many remain thoughtlessly unaware of the spirit of addiction's overall intent against the children of God. The chronic pathological behavior of addiction has in fact contrived a defiant ideology towards church doctrine and its beliefs.

This spirit has created a culture of spiritual blindness within our nation's faith communities. Because of the lack of insight and education about the assault addiction wages on the spiritual mental health of members and their families within the church, and because of the sinister progression against members of the houses of God and its neighboring members, a new social ideology towards the church has occurred. The emerging ideology is unrealistic, yet it is effective in encouraging a new perception for substance using members and for users.

The new culture in and around the church endorses the perception that service to God, weekly worship, and fellowship with other believers are no longer essential discipleship elements. It promotes the thought that for

God fearing families and communities to survive the mental, emotional, and spiritual assaults, which are the core ingredients of addiction, there is no real need to involve themselves in the community of faith. The intent of Satan's influence is to get users to believe they are just fine when in reality they are in a state of denial.

The impact of addictive socialization has led to unforeseen opportunities by Satan to dismantle established doctrines of faith that have been in place for years. Times have changed, which has resulted in ministries moving away from the regeneration of its members, and old philosophies such as, "Come as you are." The new concept, however says, "Come as you are and leave as you came!" No regeneration, no change, and no challenges!

So then, summing it all up, because the spirit which comes with addiction has no desire for the things of God, it arrives at the doorsteps of the church with a primary mission - to pull believers away from the mandated statues and commandments of God. The spirit of addiction whispers in users' ears and plants in their minds the idea that times are changing and so should the church!

History shows us that to maintain addiction and to secure a supply of substances day after day, most, if not all addicts, have to live lives of falsehood. Recently, it appears that many within our churches have also adopted deceitful ways of living. Daily, there are believers who have fallen away from dependency on God as their source of strength. They are awaking only to start the day by putting on a mask of denial. They hide behind this mask of denial to avoid being detected, or even questioned about the obvious problems addiction is causing in their walk with the Lord. For a Christian believer, it becomes even harder and more of a necessity to wear masks in order to manage their addiction and function without being discovered. These same chameleons arrive to worship on Sunday mornings covered with the stench of alcohol, marijuana, tobacco and the likes. The aroma itself confirms their double mindedness toward holiness.

Often exhausted from a night filled with hustling to get a fix, addicts, only by the grace of God, awake just in time to put on Sunday garments of praise. Unaware of the shadows that faithfully follow them into the service weekly, they integrate with other believers to avoid detection from the watchful eyes of suspecting members. Sound familiar?

As a pastor of a faith-community with the potential to be impacted by this spirit, I had a burning need to examine the question of whether or not addiction is a contributing factor preventing the growth of the church across the nation. I further stand on the principle that believers of Almighty God should be willing and motivated to ask this and other questions of reference about the state of the church of today. These questions should not be asked for discussion only, but rather, our inquiry should also come with significant goals for making the adjustments needed to protect the bride of our Lord, coupled with and outline of matching works.

I personally needed answers to what has happened to the overall morality and integrity of the church with regard to substance abuse within our ranks. I was hoping to discover a rational reason for the paramount exodus of church memberships in this millennium age. I needed to understand why there has been such a wide spread disappearance of membership in churches of all denominations. Lastly, I had become curious about whether this decrease in new members is a concern of the people of God or am I just panicking alone and over nothing.

SEATING AVAILABILITY IS NO LONGER A PROBLEM

Pew vacancies became noticeable in the late 1990's when many senior, stable, sold-out saints who were born in the early 1900's began dying off. Their transitioning and end of an era left an indelible void. These vacancies have increased in alarming numbers and have impacted significant areas of the church's physical and spiritual growth, including generational fellowship. Some churches are no longer able to tell accurate church history partially due to this phenomenon. Tenured members are waning. Additionally, where there is no housing due to plight or loss of long-term residents around the church, or where there are no viable businesses, often the value of the church facility and other properties within the immediate church community decreases. Finally, the financial stability of many ministries doesn't exist as we once knew it because of declining membership.

Because of the Devil's daily tricks against unsuspecting believers, I believe that some of our churches' memberships have suffered spiritual relapses. In some cases, members have found their way back to old methods of substance use living. I believe their hearts are still with God but their spirits have been subdued by demonic enticements of the world. This decision to fall away from church fellowship most often prevents any genuine relationship with anyone other than those who participate in their similar behavior of addiction.

The reality of our relationship with God is that it must be current and stable to keep the Devil and his imps away from our minds. One problem with engaging in addiction while serving God is that contrary spirits seek total control of users' entire being. Once the spirits have established a stronghold, it becomes difficult to shed the compulsive obsessive desire to use substances without the help of Almighty God.

I have been given a charge by God to reach out to those who are suffering with addictions - both Christian and non-Christian. I asked myself, "Why would the Father choose me for this difficult assignment?" I realize that it had to be because I have lived it! And I know firsthand that it is less difficult for a believer of God to tell a lie than for a believer to live one!

CHAPTER ONE

THE SECRET IS OUT: THE DEVIL IS A LIAR

And the Lord said, Simon, Simon, behold, Satan hath desired to have you, that he may sift you as wheat: But I have prayed for thee, that thy faith fail not: and when thou art converted, strengthen thy brethren.
Luke 22:31-32 (KJV)

THE SPIRIT OF ADDICTION

Throughout this writing, I will be using the term "spirit of addiction" because it is my belief that all substances are accompanied by some spirit form. However, let us be clear, this spirit operates in diverse forms including substances, but in other forms also, such as gambling, pornography and crime. Regardless of which spiritual agent the enemy uses, each seems to have caused members of ministries to say goodbye to their mission and to their vision of godly service.

Now more than ever in the history of the church, this spirit I call addiction is evident in congregations across the nation. In these perilous times in which we live, it can be seen from the pulpits to the parking lots of far too many congregations. This spirit has no fear of specialized denomination, special gifts, or obvious anointing. This spirit of the Devil comes only to kill, steal and destroy everything in its path.

When we reflect on how our Lord was led up into the wilderness by the Holy Spirit, we should remember that the Devil appeared to Him on several occasions. The Devil was seeking out ways to tempt Jesus with desire, fear, financial worry, and by testing Jesus's faith in every way imaginable. Know that Satan's desire was to convert our Lord over to his side of the spiritual war; but, our Lord was not tempted. However, our Lord set the example for Disciples of Christ by overcoming the enemy's temptations, walking down the mountain of trials and receiving a new gift of spiritual Power from the Father, - this Power gave Him the authority to subdue any demonic assault.

Jesus resisted the Devil, and the Devil fled. We also have the power to subdue demonic assaults; we may access that same Power by speaking the Word of God just as Jesus did, and then watch with expectation as our spoken command manifests victory over our situations.

Nevertheless, the Devil has had much success tempting and converting faithless saints of modernity. Whether we confess the reality of his invasion on our churches, families, or on our personal lives, his plan of attack against the believers of Christ is still in motion. He is still preparing multiple assaults on the church of God. His strategic goal is to overtake all of the houses of God and subdue as many saints as possible before our Lord and Savior, Jesus Christ, returns. This is why this writing is so important and centers on two separate but equal populations within the community.

SEPARATE BUT EQUAL

The two populations struggling with the same spirit of addiction are:

1) the backsliding believers, and
2) residents of churches' surrounding communities

This same spirit's collateral impact has caused a rippling effect. Many who have been afflicted with addiction have eliminated the thought of engaging in any type of service to the Lord as they are only able to concentrate on their addictive needs.

When viewed by others, it also appears that service to God and obligatory feelings toward Christ have been erased from the minds of members who are active substance users, especially from the perspective of the church and its membership. Because addiction drains the user of any ability to have any type of life beyond feeding their addiction, pursuing a spiritually healthy life is next to impossible within addiction's overpowering grasp. Compassion towards others, whether family or the church, usually diminishes during the active stages of addiction.

While it may appear that many have simply forgotten from where the Lord has brought them, a sound from heaven beckons the addictive backslider to return to God. Often these are they that find their way back to the pews. This separation from service to God did not just happen overnight. It is progressive and a process directly associated with the life draining spirit of addiction - the culprit of backsliding relative to this book.

I have been there and I have done that. I have been on both sides of this spectrum. I straddled the fence between my commitment to God and my addictive need for substances. Through the lens of addiction, I remember my backsliding years. I lived to use and I used to live! In my addictive mind, going to church and participating in any form of service was way out of the question, especially if it was going to interfere with my using time or my recuperating time. But often, amazingly, I showed up any how!

I have been involved in the movement of organized religion for over 57 years of my life. More recently, in the past 17 years of my walk with God, I have served as Pastor of New Light Family Christian Center, which is located in Detroit, Michigan. Throughout my years of worshiping God, I have noticed that the church, Christendom even, has experienced a significant doctrinal change. This change has not stemmed from a change in the doctrine itself, but rather, from people watering down the doctrine to suit their personal agendas. These interpret doctrine to often justify and explain their behavior. As many faith communities in urban America are rapidly declining, decline in memberships has impacted significant areas vital to the survival of ministry and vital to the survival of community.

For many years I have been observing and speaking with members of local congregations who have found themselves running in and out of fellowship with the church and in and out of fellowship with the Father. With so many individuals confused about their walk with God, I was led by the Holy Spirit to search for reasons so many leave the Church's covering. What I discovered was found in both the lives of Christians and non-Christians alike. What I discovered led me to the realization that substance use, along with its accompanying lifestyle, was a primary reason for the falling away in many cases. To be specific, the residue of hidden wounds from unresolved issues associated with substance abuse, either by themselves or other members of their households, led former church attendees - saved and unsaved - astray.

Developmental issues with people of God who have not yet gained closure on their personal problems are not unusual; but, if these issues are not addressed, many will turn to substance use in order to anesthetize the associated pain. If this population continues to ignore their pain ridden issues and do not seek counseling, then these are more apt to resist help in any form and are more likely to continue using - again and again.

The demons of addiction are crafty and very effective against many unsuspecting Christians. Having been unknowingly under attack by this dark spirit for so long, users become slaves and are continually subjected to demonic assaults against their minds and bodies. Because of the associated powerful torment, users are often defeated in their individual efforts to win the fight against addiction. Controlled and driven by this dark force, they voluntarily evict prayer and move in the habit instead. They become hopeless, helpless and haunted by the spirit of addiction until they end up in jail, a mental institution or the grave!

When we see believers engaging in this obsessive compulsive behavior, we also can be assured that continued use will lead them even deeper into a secular world filled with chemical dependency and sin, which is further separation from God.

Again, substance abuse is first a state of mind influenced by Satan. Unfortunately, addictive behaviors lead to building walls of denial, blocking the addicted believer's ability to connect with the Lord. To sum it all up, addiction kills the spiritual life of the user.

The process of spiritual assassination clearly perpetrated by Satan on substance abusing believers, is aimed solely at devaluing their spiritual self-concept and then mentally overthrowing them with feelings of guilt, shame, and remorse. Together these assaults result in both a spiritual and emotional shut down, followed by the addicted believer giving up on the thought of ever getting better.

OIL AND WATER NEVER MIX

Addicted believers are trying to find their way. These lost children of the Most High God have fallen into the hands of the spirit of addiction; they have become prey. These same are often searching and hoping that a Sunday message from the pulpit will offer the courage needed to resist the Devil and his imps.

Broken spirited and weary from a long night of substance abusing, many of these who make their way to church, arrive on Sundays seeking a message of hope that will somehow point their life in a safer direction. These substance abusing members are searching for relief from the horrors of the addiction lifestyle that haunts them day in and day out. They arrive desperately desiring a message, or something, anything, that will ultimately provide them the strength and skills needed to withstand the wiles of the Devil.

Secretly addicted-believing members are lying at the feet of church alters praying and desiring to hear from God on the matters of their hearts. Welcomed, these come before God emotionally trapped and clothed in demoralizing, misleading, and devaluing lifestyles that come with the wardrobe of chemical dependency. They form hope-lines together, silently reaching out for a word of faith that will utter certainty in their spirit-man, assuring that this is the day in which they will not surrender to addiction's antics. They hope to develop enough insight and courage to launch a counter assault against the adversary- the Devil and his imps.

These exact individuals who have been influenced by Satan, have found themselves hiding in the midst of the sanctuary resembling their lost community counterparts. Both groups, the backsliding believer and the community residents, unfortunately are feeling separated from God. One group feels the anxiety because of their sinful lives, their spiritual bankruptcies, and the emotional sicknesses connected to addiction's spirit. The other group feels the separation because of the devastating impact addiction has on the community.

Contrary to popular opinion, the people and the lifestyles associated with addiction, are not solely due to socio-economic conditions. Rather, because addiction can be prominent in specific American cultures, we find other preexisting factors (which I will discuss later) rising to the surface. These factors often contribute to the decaying progression of the substance abusing, compulsive users' behavior.

Because oil and water, just as good and evil cannot agree and do not mix, addictive socialization can cause spiritual division in the lives of addicted users of substances. As mentioned earlier, the Devil's influences of substance use by the children of God are designed to produce destruction in their spiritual walk, which stagnates congregations that are unaware of the attack and its impact. This is why the Lord instructs his children to abide in Him, so that He may be able to abide in them.

But, blindsided by the infiltration of addiction, many pew members suffer from Satan's unapologetic assaults against them. In some cases, the spirit of addiction will not cease until it has successfully completed its assignment, which is to render a fatal blow, a blow resulting in the death of all users, believers and nonbelievers alike.

My friends, the truth never has to defend itself. It is my sincere hope that this writing will perform its mission of telling the truth about the problem of substance abuse in the local congregations across America.

Following the commands of God to share this revelation with believers was uncomfortable for me at first; however, when I reflect on the sacrifices of our Savior, I can clearly understand that what He did for mankind surely was not comfortable. Because of Jesus Christ's example to mankind, when given an assignment by God, we too must take up our cross and begin our journey toward obedience for the sake of God's Kingdom. Just as many of the old patriarchs in the Bible, we must face the unknown with certainty that God has our back.

THE TRUTH SHALL SET YOU FREE

One of the beauties of truth is that it assists our efforts to bring change in our personal life situations. Truth, when accepted, offers an immediate opportunity to make any needed adjustments that will bring about the healthiest outcome, that is, if we are willing. Truth is printed in the heartbeat of this book, a truth that if embraced will set many captives free from the bondage of addiction.

Now you may be thinking, "What makes this pastor's story so unique?"

Stories of addiction saturate the bookshelves across the nation if not the world. You may even have a story inside of you. I, however, urge you to remember that this book is not completely about me. It is about thousands of souls trapped in and outside of Christian communities seeking a way out of their struggles with addictive agents.

This is a story which highlights hope and focuses on the possibility of the Divine intervening power from God Almighty, a Holy Ghost power that has the ability to deliver the children of God from the demonic forces of this world. This book offers assurance that anyone who believes in God can and will be saved from any demonic spirit of addiction. It is a story of how God's grace and mercy will protect and cover His chosen vessels, a story of how this same grace and mercy can and will restore all that has been lost, all that has been stolen because of this cunning spirit.

My friends, if addicted believers are to get better, there must be a spiritual intervention. To get better, users must step out of their comfort zone, cry out to God for help, and then purpose to do the will of the Father - as He has commanded. Nothing less will suffice.

Again, I am sent only to remind the church and the community that there is a spiritual power above that can provide us with grace and redemption. It is a power from God Almighty whose purpose is to protect the believer of Christ Jesus from any spiritual or earthly assault dispatched by the Devil. The beauty is when we repent and turn from our wicked ways, the promise is then offered to the unchurched, the backslider, and the believer because we are all children of God. If we return to God, He will return to us. God Almighty, through Jesus Christ, has given the world a Holy Ghost power which assures us that redemption and protection is within our reach. We only need to follow His plan of salvation to receive it.

I thank God for my deliverance, again and again, and over and over! I recognize that this book may be controversial, but controversy is good if it causes a life to be saved. The truth is not always comfortable but that does not mean that it should not be told!

SEEING IS BELIEVING - THE THOMAS SYSTEM OF BELIEF

Then He said to Thomas, Reach out your finger here, and see My hands; and put out your hand and place it in My side. Do not be faithless and disbelieving.

But stop your unbelief and believe! Jesus said to him, because you have seen Me, Thomas, do you now believe? Blessed and happy and to be envied are those who have never seen Me and yet have believed and adhere to and trusted and relied on Me.

John 20:27, 29 (Amp)

The arrival of this particular spirit in the church is calculated. We have already established that it is an assault on God's people perpetrated by the Devil, himself. An abundance of drug education and drug prevention literature exists. Countless hours have been spent in research on the overall damage caused by substance abuse. Heinous acts associated with addiction and how drug abuse literally destroys lives and eradicates any hope for posterity have been dramatized on stage and screen. Yet, some still doubt that they can actually fall victim to addiction. There are Christians who have fallen prey to addiction that testify, "I never thought it could happen to me." Like Thomas, this population possesses a "show me" attitude. The very powerful spirit of addiction uses chemical substances and other negative agents to subdue its victims and once subdued, places doubt in their minds relative to deliverance from their addiction. Some of these are your pew partners.

When this spirit attaches to the believer, it seizes its opportunity to influence the mind, body, and spirit (not soul) of these spiritually weakened believers. Many of the opportunities given to the adversary to recruit and attack believers come from both a lack of faith and from disobedience to the Word of God.

> *You are like unfaithful wives having love affairs with the world and breaking your marriage vows to God! Do you not know that being the world's friend is being God's enemy? So whosoever chooses to be a friend of the world takes his stand as an enemy of God.*
> *James 4:4 (AMP)*

My wife often shares the term of having "broken focus" when addressing our behavior as believers of Christ. Believers often lean toward the world's system as they are often moved by what they see and not by faith. God warns us all about being "lukewarm" - having an irresolute belief in Him, His abilities and His capabilities. Doubt is dangerous. Let's be clear, the enemies of God are lovers of the worldly systems created by the Devil.

> *No one can serve two masters. Either you will hate the one and love the other, or you will be devoted to the one and despise the other. You cannot serve both God and money.*
> *Matthew 6:24 (NIV)*

The backsliding of believers in the church today happens partly because of church goers' fence straddling mentality: they desire to sit in the pews, but they also desire to indulge in addictive agents. Weeks of chronic use is the evidence of addictive behaviors developing. When this phase begins, the backslider has chosen to live a life that is contrary to the will and laws of God. Ultimately, they run out the doors of the church just as fast as they ran in when they once sought refuge from the horrors and elements of a sin-filled world.

These users have become unknowingly trapped in murky, blinding, dark spiritual influences. This demonic process purposes to lead multitudes of believers back to old lifestyles and behaviors once practiced prior to accepting the Lord as their personal Savior. From club hopping and marijuana shopping, and from drinking and stinking to smoking and joking; these and other (backsliding) secular characteristics are plagued with traps set by the dark forces of Satan. Remember, the enemy's intent is to overthrow God's power by drawing the believer from the presence of their supportive church community.

Having walked the walk and talked the talk of an addicted believer years ago, I feel strongly about bringing insight to God's houses. When the spirit of addiction enters the church and begins its infestation among the saints of God, the potential damage is irreversible without God's deliverance. The perception that comes with permissible substance use in ministry, presents morality issues. When we turn our heads to issues of integrity within the ministry, what are we telling people in our congregations across America who are seeking a closer relationship with God?

We cannot afford to ignore addiction's presence.

> Brothers, if anyone is caught in any transgression, you who are spiritual should restore him in a spirit of gentleness. Keep watch on yourself, lest you too be tempted.
>
> *Galatians 6:1 (KJV)*

The Devil thrives in the spiritual warfare arena. His arsenal is equipped with both chemical and mental weapons of destruction. He is, therefore, very effective at hitting his target when employing such fleshly pleasurable agents as alcohol, drugs, gambling, illicit sex and pornography. When not addressed timely, the church's lack of a counterattack against this variety of addictions has been known to force ministries to close. Church closures ripple. Satan's continued storm of assaults on congregations and their neighboring community also has a crippling ripple effect on many families.

When we focus on chemically dependent communities across this nation, as believers of God, we surmise that these communities have been spiritually and mentally deprived, which is often due to the cultural socialization of substance abuse. Too often hopes, dreams and any possibility of surviving Satan's assault have been extinguished for these victims because of the environment in which they live.

HAD IT NOT BEEN FOR THE LORD ON MY SIDE

This book is written by the inspiration of God. It acknowledges addiction as being a spiritual death grip on the followers of Christ Jesus. It further proclaims that addiction is a well-organized spiritual attack against congregants, memberships of the local millennial congregations, and against surrounding urban communities across the nation.

Years prior to becoming the pastor of New Light, I too found myself struggling with my identity both as a Christian and as an addict. I accepted Christ at age 12 and as a direct result of my early afflictions and rebellious attitude, my life took a turn for the worse. As a youth growing up on the streets of Detroit, my hopes and dreams were put on hold during the front staging of my addiction. I certainly do not wish this to happen to anyone else.

My life was much like the experiences discussed in this book. So, in penning such, I am speaking from a place of both personal experience as well as from first-hand observations as a pastor. I am thrilled that you picked up this work. I hope and pray that it will bless you or someone else who is seeking a jump start toward their journey of deliverance from the demonic, death-seeking grip called addiction.

I have highlighted the shocking realities experienced daily behind the closed doors of many believers in Christ Jesus. I hope that through this reading I am able to assist afflicted, spiritual prisoners of war (POW's) in pulling down their denial and removing their mask of pain and suffering caused by this spirit. It is my desire to deliver avenues of relief to individuals who are seeking a way out of their struggles with addiction and the adverse affect it brings to the user, the family, and the entire body of Christ Jesus.

It is important to confront this spiritual truth head-on, thereby exposing its sinister intent for the faith community. At the risk of redundancy but embracing the power within repetition, I have established and therefore proclaim that addiction is a demonic spirit. It hides within the inner being of many afflicted church members and thus, metaphorically, causes the members to cast spiritual shadows of bondage beneath the pews in which they sit during worship hour.

So then, war has been declared and God's people are fighting back!

CHAPTER TWO
A COMMUNITY UNDER SIEGE

When two elephants are in conflict, the greater impact from the battle is found beneath their feet.
African Proverb-Author Unknown

A COMMUNITY AND A PEOPLE UNDER SIEGE

When an inner-city faith community is located in an impoverished area that has for years cultivated acceptance of addiction as part of its cultural socialization, that community breeds and thrives on this acceptance because of its substance abusing members. One thing I personally know as factual is that it is extremely hard to change a maladaptive social mindset without the help of Almighty God.

Let's face it, waking up each day only to view a landscape of burned out abandoned homes, prostitution, drug houses, medical marijuana and liquor stores, drugs and loose cigarettes being sold out of gas stations and bridge card dependency, promotes the conduct and ideology as social normality for a culture. This acceptance can, and often does, become disheartening and depressing to many living in it as well as to many across the nation who witness it. The social acceptance of the neighboring residents surrounding the physical church far too often promote a cultural rejection toward the institution of the church.

The level of rejection for the institution of the church further highlights a community's spiritual impartiality, along with its agnostic and atheistic characteristics. Continued acceptance of a substance abusing society in the faith community breeds a definitive cultural disconnect within that community. Dynamics of the community's substance abusing state also seems to affirm that the abnormal, maladaptive, sociological behavior seen in the surrounding areas of churches is the accepted norm within the community.

It is this classic dysfunctional conditioning that allows a community to become tolerant of the landscape in which it moves in and out of daily. What one might see as catastrophic, others see as just another day in the hood. It can become harder to see the dysfunction of darkness without the proper understanding or benefit of experiences revealing how something could appear if given more light.

The collateral damage of the community's acceptance of their state often produces consequences within its boundaries, inside and outside the walls of churches. Furthermore, if the social decay of the community is not addressed, these negative circumstances will over time impact both the community and the churches.

Although my concerns are with addicted church members, the surrounding community also suffers from chronic chemical dependency behaviors. Both populations generate two immediate areas of concern:

1) Often churches suffer due to their inability to develop a stronger congregation derived from its neighboring community and

2) Because of addictive patterned lifestyles, generational substance abuse develops along with passing down maladaptive social behaviors which again, shows acceptance of the addictive lifestyles within the community by the church.

No longer do we have the luxury of focusing primarily on those who we believe are thieves inside of ministries today. Yes, historically, communities have unfairly condemned the character of male pastors without cause in many situations. The indictment claimed that male pastors' persona was reflective of a pimp, a swindler, and a false prophet, to say the least. Despite all the dedicated service these pastors have provided to the church and to the community, in most cases, these claims were unsubstantiated.

In this millennial age, however, churches are hit with new theft concerns. Individual addicts within the community who are constantly breaking in homes and businesses stealing metal pipes, copper lines and wiring, present a rising dilemma for the church and its community. If thieves discover that these items aren't obtainable, then other significant equipment needed for the ministry to operate is often stolen. Sadly, these essential items are stolen daily from churches because of the associated pilfering spirits that accompany addictive behaviors.

Once an unwritten creed, the "do not touch the church" oath within the community, has now changed to "all is fair game." The church has become a shopping mall for thieves seeking ways to find revenue to feed the demonic spirit. Let us be real, what other group would steal from the House of God other than certified imps? Who and what else would benefit by destroying the churches of God?

Just as the Devil went into Judas to sell out Christ, so his spirit enters into those who are afflicted with addiction.

Morals and integrity have no place in the world of substance abuse because addiction destroys anyone and everything it touches. Thus, ministries and its memberships are impacted by the 'take want you want' dogma established by these imps. Coincidently, again, what nourishes these spiritual attacks against the church in the community is a socially shared system, which promotes the views and opinions that service to God, weekly worship, and fellowship with other believers is not necessary to develop and maintain a lasting relationship with the Creator.

These imps are most successful because many urban communities no longer take personal ownership for the churches in their demographic area. This relational dismantling of communities is not happening by accident; these are calculated strategies employed by Satan. In fact, a part of the Devil's arsenal is that he establishes pictorial defeat of the ruined areas around the community of faith.

Although much of the questionable social activities mentioned seem to be happening outside the church walls, we must remember the essential segment this perspective is focusing on: the spiritual assault that the spirit of addiction has had on both the church and surrounding communities. Moreover, when looking at the destruction addiction causes, there are crucial spiritually debilitating events happening inside the congregation as well.

One of the primal behaviors of addicted individuals is deceit. Addicted believers live lives of falsehood daily. Now, when referencing the addicted believer inside the church, we find that this group has managed over time to build defense walls when addressing problems of addiction with anyone in the church community. Sadly, these defensive walls (of denial) have separated them from God Himself. These chemically induced barriers have caused addicted believers to disconnect with the Lord because of their allegiance to the spirit of addiction.

Often because of their commitment to the intense social activities of addiction, many users' lives resemble an amusement park roller-coaster with ups and downs, twists and turns, and around and around behavior. Because of the illicit activities that accompany the acquisition of substances, self-concept for many has been overthrown by guilt, shame and regret, greatly similar to what is exhibited in the lives of backsliders and non-believers.

When we visit the creation story in the book of Genesis, we can clearly ascertain that the original goal of the Devil is the same today as in those early Garden of Eden days. We can surmise that the Devil has one career mission: to attempt acts of evil toward all of mankind endeavoring to destroy God's plan for Creation.

Do not be fooled by any means. Satan is not afraid of attacking the believer with spirits of addiction. In fact, the demons of addiction are crafty and effective. However, I may need to point out that there are many believers who clearly understand the tricks played on the children of God by Satan. These believers have utilized the spirit of wisdom over him and his imps and have escaped his traps. Because of their continued relationship with the Father, this group recognizes the snares set for them and manage to escape the death-grip of addiction. The problem is that there are far too many other victims who do not have this freedom experience to report.

I am saddened to say that there are believers in our Lord and Savior who wake each day by the grace of God, and start their daily routines by putting on a social mask of denial. Having the need to hide the pains associated with needing a fix to get started, or to get them through the work day, or to make it through the night, is hard for many to endure.

ONE BAND. ONE BEAT. ONE SOUND.

Because most communities are well-knitted, whereas communication and issues within families are often disclosed and later passed around from house to house, it is certainly known by most within the community that at the end of the work week many addicted residents begin a weekend of celebration with their substances of choice. If the truth were to be told, these are the same residents who take on the chameleon traits at the Sunday morning worship services. Ironically, these same disguised spiritual giants report to God full of denial on Sunday mornings. Because of the chronic use of substances, while even in worship, the spirit of addiction has covered them with the stench of double-mindedness and it has saturated their very being.

Because of the history behind the spirit of addiction and the destructive intent it brings, it can no longer be considered a small issue. And if this concern were isolated, we might be able to find ways to make adjustments that would benefit the churches and the communities over time.

This, however, is a major issue and it has caused major damage to members in the church and community residents outside the reaches of the congregation. I believe this spirit to possibly be one of the most difficult assaults on the church of God today. With the large number of churches shutting their doors daily and with pastors leaving pulpits because of exhaustion and loss of faith, one can only ask the question, "If not the cultural socialization of addicted lifestyles, then what else has impacted the church in the millennium age?"

THE SPIRIT OF ADDICTION MUST SUBMIT

In the gospel according to Mark 5:1-20, Jesus went into the country of Gadarenes and was approached by a man filled with an unclean spirit. When Christ asked the demon-filled man his name, the man answered,

My name is Legion: for we are many.
Mark 5:9 (KJV)

To fully understand this scriptural message, you must understand the sequence of events.

> 1) Jesus is always intentional. The story helps us to see and understand the power of God in His Son. Jesus goes to a place where the dead are housed and are overseen by a man with many unclean spirits. When the unclean spirits recognized Jesus through the eyes of the demonic possessed man, they ran to Him and asked not to be tormented.

> 2) Jesus commands the unclean spirits to come out of the man. Jesus didn't bargain or sweetly ask, but rather, He commanded the demons by His authority to immediately vacate the man's person.

3) Jesus asked, "What is your name?" The demon possessed man answered, "Legion; for we are many."

All spirits have names, one of which we referenced throughout is "addiction," and every spirit must submit to the authority of God given through the Name of Jesus. For by no other means can we be saved from the spiritual attack of the Devil, including the spirit of addiction. This spirit, too, must bow down to the authority of the Lord.

Keep in mind it is never too late for God. He heals and delivers so that He alone can get the glory!

In the gospel according to John, it records Lazarus rising from the dead after having been dead four days. Jesus shows up, prays to the Father, gives Him thanks for the next miracle, and raises Lazarus from the grave for the glory of God. You see, it does not matter to God what your spiritual stronghold is, but by Jesus' name they must loose you and let you go! In both circumstances the Lord commanded both the spirt of legions and the spirit of death to loose and depart these men. The good news is that they did obey and all must obey!

Getting honest and examining behaviors of members of our church congregation is vitally important for ministry stability. We can no longer waste time and energy with self-deception when reviewing the church membership rolls.

When we are straightforward about the diversity we have in our weekly services, then we can begin to accept that many of the people in our worship services are hurting and temporarily disconnected from God. Many are spiritually lost due to the spirit of addiction's impact on their families and on their personal lives. The church's acceptance of this major issue can only aid in motivating and leading the church to develop more programming designed to assist and not resist the communities we serve.

A CHURCH UNDER SEIGE

The scripture records in the Apostle Paul's letter to Rome these words:

> *For ye have not received the spirit of bondage again to fear; but ye have received the Spirit of adoption whereby we cry, Abba, Father.*
>
> *Romans 8:15 (KJV)*

Most pastors who counsel others agree that many come to pastoral care seeking answers and prayers for deliverance from the impact addiction has on their households. The truth is if one house is hurting in the church, then the entire church should feel their pain. Churches must ask the following questions when trying to address the multiple needs of their membership who are addicted:

1) Are there members in the local congregation where I worship who appear to have substance-seeking behavior?

2) When in counseling, do members report going places where they know drugs and alcohol abuse is prevalent?

3) Do these members report a compulsion to engage in problematic behaviors in increasing episodes, which include gambling?

4) Do members report more time focused on getting high and less time seeking God for solutions?

5) Do members report that addiction seems to be the reason they use substances?

6) Have some reported that they "live to use" and they "use to live"?

7) Do members report they have lost touch with important aspects of their lives, such as church, friends, work, school, health and family responsibilities because of their use and addictive behavior?

If the members are saying "yes" to these questions then there is strong evidence that they are being influenced by the spirit of addiction.

EVERYTHING MUST CHANGE BUT SOMETHINGS ALWAYS STAY THE SAME

Changes in the demographics of our church roll in the last ten years or so is a hard reality that must be faced when working with the unchurched membership within our congregation. Because of the shift in the secular world, systems in the church have been impacted by familiar spirits.

This social reality is big enough issue alone for the congregation to take on. With its current roster of substance abusers exhibiting a new wave of mental health issues within the church, however, we still have a spiritually mandated commission to disciple. It is our Christian duty to aid in the spiritual development of transferred members regardless of what baggage with which they arrive at the ministry's door steps.

Arriving at the ministry with undisclosed afflictions stemming from addictive patterns of behavior, substance abusers are quick to share the uncertainty of their relationship with God. Fragile in their faith, this group has multiple doctrinal beliefs and show up with the hope of somehow merging them all in a way that will let the abuser maintain both a secular and Christian lifestyle.

Replanted from one church congregation to another, the sincerity of these members, as unfair as it may sound, is often challenged because they lack a desire for holiness. Many come looking for a microwave worship experience. We know now that the spirit of addiction steals, kills and destroys the hope of the user. So then, unfortunately, with this membership comes issues of spiritual defeatism. This may occur because of their moving from church to church throughout the course of their addiction. Often these transplants are without solid Biblical roots or a long-term understanding of their relational walk with God.

Not all arrive confused. A select few arrive from other congregations where their behaviors were discovered. They often move their membership with the excuse that it was something about the church or something about the pastor that they did not like. But more often than not, we learn sooner or later, that their addiction was discovered; so, out of anger, frustration and bitterness for having been exposed, these ran from the opportunity of deliverance. The spirit of addiction often takes on the appearance of bitterness, especially when its shadow has been seen.

And the Egyptians made the children of Israel to serve with rigour: And they made their lives bitter with hard bondage.
Exodus 1:13-14a (KJV)

Without fail the spirit of addiction will put the user under the authority of Satan each and every time they engage in addictive activities. It becomes Satanic captivity, imprisonment, and slavery. For the record, let me add that the spirit of addiction operates with its companion, "the spirit of bondage." Together they hunt like a small pack of wolves seeking out helpless prey to devour for their pleasure. These spiritual companions can and will bring any victim to their knees if allowed access. These forces produce blindness and brokenness in the spirit of the user. Anything broken has but two options: to be thrown away, or, to be restored to its original state.

For there shall arise false Christs, and false prophets, and shall shew great signs and wonders; insomuch that, if it were possible, they shall deceive the very elect.
Matthew 24:24 (KJV)

When our members surrender to the spirit of addiction they automatically accept the spirit of bondage as a bonus affliction. Surrendering to the demonic forces of Satan subjects addicts to whatever demands and practices the

Devil desires. In fact, the spirit of addiction becomes the puppeteer and the user becomes the puppet.

Let us now look at the impact that this spirit of addiction has on the user's mind, body and spirit.

THE MIND

Indeed, the battleground with any demonic spirit begins in the mind. So, if there is any place to look for the presence of the Devil's influence you need not look any further than the mind. The Devil loves (if such a thing exists for him) to take up space in the mind of the believer. The only defensive strategy available to believers is in the power of the Word of God. Our source of continued power is the relationship we have with the Holy Spirit and the Word of God. The more we study the Word of God the sharper our minds become. The more we come to understand the Word of God through the assistance of the Holy Spirit, the more we acquire spiritual weapons to fight the spirit of addiction.

Keep in mind that to secure the power, we must submit to daily prayer. A prayer life is a life filled with communication with God. I have internalized my walk with the Lord through prayer as my petition to God. Through study of the Word of God, I receive answers to my petition. Finally, I would appeal to you to understand that these two major ingredients of study and prayer is enhanced and works out best when the element of praise is added. More importantly, this was the very recipe I used for my personal deliverance from the spirit of addiction. You see, the blood of Jesus is our only defense. To activate the deliverance properties of the blood of our Savior, we must stay focused on Calvary. We must praise!

The Devil understands this recipe perfectly! That's why he has crafted the technique of getting into the mind of his prey and influencing them through the enticement of billboards, radio, TV, internet, and other media outlets. He wants his prey to see the messages and then receive the negative results conveyed through the messages he places in their minds. The spirit of addiction encourages this whole heartedly when we begin to see that everything around us promotes addiction.

It is important that we look at a couple tactics used by Satan today.

First, he uses specific mental messages centered on the obsession for the use of different substances. The user thinks only about using their substance of choice. How, when, where, and what are the primary thoughts at this point. The users *EGO - (ease God out)* thought kicks in. No thought of prayer, fasting or reading the Word for deliverance is on the agenda.

Second, he sends mental messages that promote the compulsion side of the spirit of addiction. This is the most intense part of his attack against the user. In this stage, the user begins to consume the substance provided by Satan and his imps and then discovers an inability to stop using it once they have begun. In these two acts, you can see how Satan steals our serenity by swapping it with SIN-renity!

Most rebel against the term "sin" when discussing addiction. However, it is significant to understand that the common denominator used by Satan in all his chemical attacks is sin, and there is really no need to dress it up: it is separation from God and it is simply *SIN (Seeking Inadequate Nurturing)*!

Times and cultures have indeed changed. There is a pill, a drink, a meal for every physical, mental and emotional dilemma in our lives. One of the greatest challenges before the church today is the legalization of harmful addicting substances, including alcohol, marijuana and deadly pharmacological drugs. Let me be clear, the use of some God-made and man-altered chemicals are essential to our well being here on earth. However, we must remember that anything we worship other than God Almighty is an offense and is against the mandate of God.

The Bible records:

> *And God spoke all these words, saying, I am the Lord thy God, which have brought thee out of the land of Egypt, out of the house of bondage. Thou shalt have no other gods before me. Thou shalt not bow down thyself to them, nor serve them: for I the Lord thy God am a jealous God, visiting the iniquity of the fathers upon the children unto the third and fourth generation of them that hate me;*
> *Exodus 20:1-2, 5 (KJV)*

The Bible speaks about a need to have total control over one's mind.

> *Let this mind be in you, which was also in Christ Jesus:*
> *Philippians 2:5 (KJV)*

We have a definite need to guard our thoughts because,

> *"For as he thinketh in his heart, so is he: Eat and drink, saith he to thee, but his heart is not with thee.*
> *Proverbs 23:7 (KJV)*

The spirit of addiction totally consumes its victims. The oppressive components of the spirit of addiction celebrate the destruction of lives, family, communities, and definitely houses of worship. Churches have trained, security ministries; many have installed expensive security camera devices and monitoring system. However, it would appear at first sight that no security system, mechanical or human, is able defend itself against the sinister assault launched by the spirit of addiction on the congregants that it attacks.

Just as modern terrorists, addiction takes on its form by way of spiritual identity theft. It comes in under the spiritual radar and attacks its victim before they are able to discover the threat on their life. This seductive spirit specializes in stealing the focus of its prey and slowing down their ability to react to devices launched against the mind of the user. When a person's mind is preoccupied with chemical substances, their ability to react is often disabled. Thus, reaction time is slowed, delayed or altogether stopped, making it almost impossible to render appropriate decisions about life and spiritual concerns.

Consequently, if you cannot move out of the way of these spiritual attacks because of your slowed, delayed or altogether stopped reaction time, you may have acquired spiritual paralysis. Paralysis accompanies the behavior associated with this spirit. The local church must always stay focused on the tactics used by Satan and remember that the mind is the battle ground for spiritual victories. We must rest in the certainty—

> *For the weapons of our warfare are not carnal, but mighty through God to the pulling down of strongholds.*
>
> *2 Corinthians 10:4 (KJV)*

The Word of God instructs us to resist the Devil and ignore him! Regardless of what the enemy uses against the people of God, we are instructed by God Almighty to use the correct weaponry as established by the Lord. As a church, we must protect the mindset of our congregants at all costs!

THE SHADOW BENEATH THE PEWS

Let me point out this scenario. Every church at one time or another has been blessed with new members joining the ministry. These new congregants are sincere about turning their heart to the Lord. Generally, the problem is not a matter of the heart but a matter of mind conditioning. So many Christians are bound by addictive behaviors; they want to be free, but don't know how to attain freedom. The issues for the church and its addicted membership are the following:

> 1. Before one can overcome any addiction, one must first admit that there is a problem and that it is *SIN*. That seems to be so hard when substances are all you know. James's epistle instructs us to—

> *Confess your faults to one another, and pray for one another, that you may be healed. The effective, fervent prayer of the righteous man accomplishes much.*
> *James 5:16 (KJV)*

2. A quality decision that one will do whatever is necessary to be free from this ungodly behavior must be made. However, many report that their decisions are made by the spirit of addiction. Be not alarmed, there is a plan to freedom outlined in James 4:7:

Submit yourselves therefore to God. Resist the Devil, and he will flee from you.

My friend, understanding how to submit to God is a must in order to get His undivided attention! One problem is addicted believers have so much guilt, shame, and remorse- all ploys of the Devil. They also suffer with a personal sense of self-importance, which is to say they often believe that the world evolves around them.

Needless to say, these emotional roller coasters make it hard for addicts to trust the process of deliverance. This emotional bondage prevents the addicted believer from seeking God and it delays their opportunity to receive grace through His Son, Jesus. Humility is not optional when seeking help from the Lord.

The addicted believer fails to accept the fact that they must ask God for forgiveness if the process of deliverance is ever to begin. That is what confessing our sins to God is all about. Seeking His forgiveness and believing He will honor our act of surrendering is significant to the process of deliverance.

If we confess our sins, He is faithful and just to forgive us our sins, and cleanse us from all unrighteousness.
1 John 1:9 (KJV)

For us to fully understand spiritual deliverance we must do specific things to show forth effort and our desire to be healed. Below are a few simple suggestions alone with scriptural support laid out for you that will strengthen your renewed relationship with the Creator.

1. Make every effort to seek out and join a Bible believing church. "So then faith comes by hearing, and hearing by the word of God" (Romans 10:17).

2. Surround yourself with supportive people. "Do not be deceived: 'Bad company corrupts good morals'" (1 Corinthians 15:33).

3. Don't take on stress or worry. "Be anxious for nothing, but in everything, by prayer and supplication with gratitude, make your requests known to God " (Philippians 4:6).

4. Take control of your thoughts by: "Casting down imaginations and every high thing that exalts itself against the knowledge of God, bringing every thought into captivity to the obedience of Christ. (2 Corinthians 10:5).

5. Bible reading is a must to aid in the cleansing of yourself spiritually so "That He might sanctify and cleanse it with the washing of water by the word." (Ephesians 5:26).

6. Fast and pray for deliverance. "He said to them, 'this kind cannot come out except by prayer and fasting'" (Mark 9:29).

7. Pray in the Spirit to encourage yourself. "But you, beloved, build yourselves up in your most holy faith. Praying in the Holy Spirit" (Jude 1:20).

What substance users must come to understand is that the spirit of addiction is out to control and destroy. To be free from its attachment, an addict must decide to do whatever it takes to be delivered from its destructive power. If you practice the aforementioned suggestions on a daily basis, eventually you will break free from the sinful and addictive behaviors. The enemy will flee from you and the freedom you so desire will be yours.

One of the issues that prevents deliverance, starts with the environment in which we associate. It is more likely that we will continue in our addictive behavior when we continue to associate with other addicted individuals. Because the addictive believer lives a double life, the stronger personality will always win. In spite of what we have learned thus far, coming out from among the unclean things is top priority.

THE SPIRITUAL IMPACT OF AN ADDICTIVE CULTURAL SOCIALIZATION

Let us imagine that a neighborhood has 20 homes per street block. Out of those 20 homes, five have been impacted by the spirit of addiction, and 15 or 75% of the homes on the block have not. Of course, this is a low number in comparison to an average inner-city block, but for the sake of explanation, let's use these low numbers for discovery.

If we consider a 10-block radius surrounding the average church community, there are 200 homes within the church's reach. Now, that would probably be an awesome dream for a well-trained evangelism team. However, let's look again. Remember that five out of 20 or 25% are impacted by the spirit of addiction.

Now, we should understand that out of the prospect of recruiting 200 families for the ministry, 50 of the homes in this scenario have been impacted by the spirit of addiction. Are you beginning to see the magnitude of the impact the spirit of addiction has on a community?

This is to say that 50 houses out of 200 within the church's reach for evangelism have problems associated with the spirt of addiction. And then these same families become part of the local church, bringing with them their mental health challenges of undisclosed addictions. Are things starting to add up?

Using the term "mental health" may appear harsh; however, issues of chemical dependency and addiction fall right smack in the middle of mental health diagnoses. Furthermore, the reality of the state of many faith communities - when we accept the shadow beneath the pews - may sometimes resemble the crisis triage unit of local hospitals across this nation. Now you can see the concern. As members of the body of Christ, we must make the necessary adjustments to assist those in crisis, in need, in bondage, in denial, and battling a war for their spirit. If one person out of the 50 homes mentioned above can be affected by Satan's spirit of addiction, then many other family members can also be influenced. The problem continues to grow until the entire community is destroyed.

The question is, "how would the above-mentioned families survive the Devil's attack on their entire household without help from the church community?" These shadows are formed from various spirits of addiction and are now cast beneath the pews in many local churches across the globe. These shadows have become a hard reality for many congregations as well as pastors.

It is a reality that needs to be addressed sooner rather than later! When we honestly examine the situation within our memberships with special attention on those members who are addicted believers, we can only conclude that addiction has robbed them of their freedom, control over their lives, and their relationship with God.

For the sake of clarity, this is not the place to point the finger of judgement at any of our members; that is the Lord's job. However, this is the place to begin thinking about discipleship work of saving the lost. This is not a new epiphany. It is the duty and obligation of the house of worship because the Devil comes as a thief in the night and he purposes to terminate all that he touches. We, at the house of God, should be on guard at all times in our walk with the Lord. Because the spirits which convoy addiction work both in the flesh, and in the spirit, we must stay on guard. I can't stress this importance enough! As believers, we may have the knowledge of the road to salvation, but there may be times when we fail to travel it!

GET READY TO MOVE

The decisions we make in life are based on the ideas which we have already accepted. Wrong ideas lead to wrong conclusions. The most important decision we will ever make involves our relationship with God and His Son, Jesus Christ. This decision will affect every other decision we make in life as a church standing on the promises of God.

We cannot forget the importance of understanding that,

> *"...the god of this world hath blinded the minds of them which believe not, lest the light of the glorious gospel of Christ, who is the image of God, should shine unto them."*
>
> 2 Corinthians 4:4 (KJV)

Remember Nicodemus? He was a religious ruler. He came to Jesus one night seeking answers to questions about his personal relationship with God. He needed to understand where he stood with the Father. He listened as Jesus said to him:

> *Verily, Verily, I say unto thee, except a man be born again, he cannot see the kingdom of God. Nicodemous said unto him, how can a man be born when he is old?*
>
> John 3:3-4 (KJV)

Jesus explains that he was speaking not of a physical rebirth. He went on to say to Nicodemous,

> *For God sent not his Son into the world to condemn the world; but that the world through him might be saved. He that believeth on him is not condemned: but he that believeth not is condemned already, because he hath not believed in the name of the only begotten Son of God.*
> *John 3; 17-18 (KJV)*

We must recognize and reject Satan's lies and spirits, so that they do not keep us from accepting the living, eternal Son of God, Jesus Christ, our Redeemer and Deliverer.

CHAPTER THREE

WE WERE CREATED IN THE IMAGE OF GREATNESS

And the Lord God formed man of the dust of the ground and breathed into his nostrils the breath of life; and man became a living soul.

Genesis 2:7 (KJV)

THE BODY

We find these words in the story of creation:

Then God said, 'Let Us make man in Our image, according to Our likeness; and let them rule over the fish of the sea and over the birds of the sky and over the cattle and over all the earth, and over every creeping thing that creeps on the earth.' God created man in His own image, in the image of God He created him; male and female He created them.

Genesis 1:26-27 (NASB)

God intended for us to be free from any attacks on our mind, body, spirit and soul.

The creation story supports and indicates that there was peace upon the earth and that God was in control of everything He created. According to the Bible, God made mankind to be different from all the rest of creation; so, He made us in His image. As God exists in the form of the Trinity (Father, Son and Holy Spirit) so man is fashioned in three parts (body, soul and spirit).

In the clearest of illustrations from Scripture, the Apostle Paul writes of these divisions:

> *Now may the God of peace Himself sanctify you entirely; and may your spirit and soul and body be preserved complete, without blame at the coming of our Lord Jesus Christ.*
> *1 Thessalonians 5:23 (NASB)*

Man is made up of the physical - the body; that is understood. Yet, he is also made up of intangible aspects such as the soul, spirit, mind, heart, intellect, will, emotions, and conscience. Each of these aspects has their own responsibility and collectively, these aspects make up the whole personality.

Satan understands that if mankind, through every aspect of his being, would truly connect with the Father, our destiny would be fully understood, our kindship would be accepted and our walk with God would be reflected - in all we do.

The Bible makes it clear that the soul and spirit are the primary aspects of the physical, but ultimately important to our eternal heavenly destination. These immaterial characteristics exist beyond the physical lifespan of the human body; they are eternal. Jesus Christ our Savior came that we may have the right to eternal life with our Creator. While the body is the physical container that holds these elements on this earth, the body (Greek, "soma") is the entire material or physical structure of a human being; it is the physical part of a person.

The Apostle Paul writing to the Romans again, connects the body, the mind (soul) and the spirit.

> *Therefore, I urge you, brethren, by the mercies of God, to present your bodies a living and holy sacrifice, acceptable to God, which is your spiritual service of worship. And do not be conformed to this world, but be transformed by the renewing of your mind, so that you may prove what the will of God is, that which is good and acceptable and perfect.*
> *Romans 12:1-2 (NASB)*

For you have been bought with a price: therefore, glorify God in your body.
1 Corinthians 6:20 (NASB)

When attached to believers, the spirit of addiction destroys lives from the outside-in. Church members, close friends and family members of addicted believers are often the first to notice problems and seek pastoral or other professional help. Many times, the addicted individual does not realize the severity of the problem or denies it. Some signs can go unnoticed, such as isolation, poor church attendance, job loss, family problems and law violations, such as citations for driving under the influence of alcohol or any other substance.

This section of the text will explore and submit the medical models for the spirit of addiction and its impact on the individual, the community and the church. When the body is in a state of dependence, physical manifestations can include symptoms of withdrawal, injuries from accidents, or blackouts. This section will further aid us in understanding the spirit of addiction on the human body, and list ways to lift the blinders on those who have refused to accept the condition in which addiction has left them, a friend, or a family member.

Perhaps the following information may clear the air on many of the questions about people in your community or those in your congregation whom you suspect may be suffering from the spirit of addiction.

The American Psychiatric Association (APA) has developed strict criteria for the clinical diagnosis of abuse and dependence as outlined in The Diagnostic and Statistical Manual-IV, also known as the DSM-IV. The DMS-IV defines *abuse* as "a maladaptive pattern of substance use leading to clinically significant impairment or distress" (APA, 2000). From the medical perspective, addiction is defined as "experiencing at least three or more of the following criteria in a 12-month period":

> 1. Recurrent substance use resulting in a failure to fulfill major role obligations at work, school, home (e.g., repeated absences or poor work performance related to substance use; substance-related absences, suspensions, or expulsions from school; neglect of children or household)
>
> 2. Recurrent substance use in situations in which it is physically hazardous (e.g., driving an automobile or operating a machine when impaired by a substance)
>
> 3. Recurrent substance-related legal problems (e.g., arrests for substance-related disorderly conduct)

4. Continued substance use despite having persistent or recurrent social or interpersonal problems caused or exacerbated by the effects of the substance (e.g., arguments with spouse about consequences of intoxication, physical fights).

These symptoms have not yet met the criteria for Substance Dependence for the patterns of substance use as referenced above.

Most often, abuse is diagnosed in individuals who recently began using alcohol or other illicit substances. Over time, abuse can progress to dependence. However, some are able to use substances for long periods without developing a dependence. Dependence is suspected when substance use is accompanied by signs of the following:

- Abuse
- Compulsive drinking behavior
- Tolerance
- Withdrawal

DSM-IV defines **dependence** as "a maladaptive pattern of substance use, leading to clinically significant impairment or distress, as manifested by three (or more) of the following, occurring at any time in the same 12-month period":

1. Tolerance, as defined by either a need for markedly increased amounts of the substance to achieve intoxication or desired effect, or markedly diminished effect with continued use of the same amount of substance

2. Withdrawal, as manifested by either the characteristic withdrawal syndrome from the substance, or taking the same (or a closely related) substance to relieve or avoid withdrawal symptoms

3. The substance is often taken in larger amounts or over a longer period than was intended

4. There is a persistent desire or unsuccessful attempts to cut down or control substance use

5. A great deal of time is spent in activities to obtain the substance, use the substance, or recover from its effects

6. Important social, occupational or recreational activities are given up or reduced because of substance use

7. The substance use is continued despite knowledge of having a persistent or recurrent physical or psychological problem that is likely to have been

caused or exacerbated by the substance (e.g., continued drinking despite recognition that an ulcer was made worse by alcohol consumption).

Dependence is also demonstrated by symptoms such as withdrawal, injuries from accidents, or blackouts.

Remembering that the medical model has much merit, I use it daily in my walk with God when reaching out to others. Whether or not it is used to determine the stages of one's active use of substances, the spirit of addiction can surface in several patterns of behavior that are not associated with chemical use. This spirit feeds off anything that pulls us away from God.

Now, with the hope that we have a fuller understanding of the medical model's assessment of addiction on the body, I have now assumed the challenge of reviewing the spiritual impact of the spirits associated with addiction.

THE SOUL

The creation account in Genesis 2:7 states that man was created as a "living soul." The soul (Greek "psyche") consists of the mind (which includes the conscience), will and emotions. The soul and the spirit are mysteriously tied together and make up what the Scriptures call the "heart." In Proverbs 4:23 the writer declares, "Watch over your heart with all diligence, for from it flow the springs of life" (NASB). We see here that the "heart" is central to our emotions and will. This is why the Devil is so adamant about keeping the children of God oppressed and depressed. He wants to keep us heartbroken so that he can do as he will in our minds.

The author of Ecclesiastes records, "He has planted eternity in the human heart" (3:11, NLT). Then, Apostle Paul records the following about non-believers:

> *But a natural man does not accept the things of the Spirit of God, for they are foolishness to him; and he cannot understand them, because they are spiritually appraised.*
> *1 Corinthians 2:14 (NASB)*

Finally, the Spirit (Greek "Pneuma"):

> *Moses and Aaron, "fell upon their faces, and said, O God, God of the spirits of all flesh, when one man sins, will you be angry with the entire congregation?*
> *Numbers 16:22 (KJV)*

This verse names God as the God of the spirits that are possessed by all humanity. Notice also that it mentions the flesh (body) of all mankind, connecting it with the spirit.

Another key verse that describes the separation between soul and spirit is Hebrews 4:12:

> *For the word of God is living and active and sharper than any two-edged sword, and piercing as far as the division of soul and spirit, of both joints and marrow, and able to judge the thoughts and intentions of the heart.*

This is, again, why we have to guard our hearts. We see in this passage of Scripture that the soul and spirit can be divided and that it is the Word of God that pierces our heart to bring the division of soul and spirit, something that only God can do.

As human beings, we live eternally as a spirit, we have a soul, and we dwell in a body. We can rejoice with the Psalmist and declare,

> *For You formed my inward parts; You wove me in my mother's womb. I will give thanks to You, for I am fearfully and wonderfully made; Wonderful are Your works, and my soul knows it very well.*
> *Psalm 139:13-14 (NASB)*

Now that we have reviewed the impact of addiction on the mind, body, soul and spirit, we have the tools to more fully understand Satan's desires to tear God's Kingdom down; if need be, one member and one church at a time. We now understand the weapons of Satan's warfare are CARNAL, which he uses to buildup strongholds against the children of God.

SEND ME LORD, I'LL GO

Addiction is a sensitive issue in the church. However, if we do not address the spiritual weapons inside of Satan's military arsenal we might as well surrender now! Sadly, I am aware that many in the church community look down on those who have had to suffer with the affliction of addiction. Often it may appear to the addicted that churches, which are supposed to be open, compassionate and willing to aid these individuals in getting help, far too often chase them away with their judgmental attitudes and "better-than thou" personas.

The Bible records several moments in its history where our Savior healed people who had been afflicted with sickness, and with each deliverance, He presented questions about belief and faith. As a result of the person's faith, their healing was given to them. The fact remains that within the linings of healing stories, we find a continual issue with the local church people. Issues of doctrine and often through their own insecurities, the locals found offensive what Jesus did for the sick among Him, and, that He performed acts of healing and deliverance on the Sabbath.

Much like church policies today, addicted believers are escorted away from mainstream and placed in rooms away from the masses only to be told to come back during the week for help. These and other gestures come out of an uncertainty of the visitor's motive. On both sides of the argument is concern of harm. Trust issues are a major concern for people afflicted with chemical dependency. Which is why, when seeing the reaction and handling of anyone with an addiction, it is so hard for chemically dependent believers to come out of the closet.

In many urban churches we discover the alarming reality more often than not - from the pulpit to the parking lot – that there is serious and devastating spiritual denial about the presence of addiction in the ranks of the congregation. Because of status and titles, we find that the pathology is often concealed behind positions held in the church by tenured leadership members. These spiritual chameleons refuse to address the problems within their homes such as substance abuse and alcoholism associated with years of secretive drunkenness.

Let's face it, sometimes our church parishioners are comprised of the elite from outside the faith community walls. Each one seems to be in control as they function in their own dysfunctional world of deception. As we have come to recognize, quite often high-visibility careers and elitist positions are extremely stressful. Working in such occupations can be demanding and overwhelming for many, which in some situations, insert additional stressors on the home and on one's personal life. Keeping it all together may seem to be impossible without a drink here and there. Consequently, many run to substances instead of running to the Lord for aid in relief of stress.

In the clinical field of addiction, stress can cause the individual to develop a desire to use substances. Stress serves as a trigger and activation of triggers lead the sufferer to find some form of relief. Because of the high stress of day-to-day living, many within the millennium faith community partake in bar hopping and club dropping as a personal right. Addicted believers are filling the local bars, pubs, and lounges during "happy hour" in alarming numbers, especially after a long week of dealing with the high demands of the job, the home, and life as a whole.

Yes, this ideology may be true if we are not walking in the Spirit. However, it is important that we stay away from unclean environments if we are going to truly grow in the Lord. Life is not easy. When we are headed on a pathway of destruction and cannot find a way out, it can become even harder to see the light, especially for the believer. God does not operate in double-mindedness. The spirit of addiction not only destroys our relationship with God the Father but it has its effect on the user's personal life as well.

The user's family may have washed their hands of dealing with the user. He or she may become unemployable, then social decay sets in resulting in friendships dwindling down to none. Finally, one finds oneself in a place of being sick and tired of just being sick and tired. One gets to a place where there is nowhere else to turn but back to God!

Many churches today contend with accepting members who are not willing to do the things required by God to truly become born again believers. This compromising ideology, making ends meet for the benefit of the budget, is killing the mission of the church of God. There is no question that in recent years of the church, pastors have turned their heads to obvious social issues that are sitting directly in front of them, casting shadows under the pews. Do you remember the old saying "what you see is what you get"? That saying does not seem to be applicable to the people of God in recent years.

People come to church seeking spiritual entertainment and refuse to engage in any act that would require commitment to any ministry. Sadly, they will not pray, evangelize, fast, tithe, or submit to the God-given authority of leadership. So, if the number of members on a church's roster does not accurately determine individual spiritual transformation, then how do we truly measure Christian growth in ministry? The truth is, as a result of their personal addictions, many Christians in our local faith communities cannot commit to anything at this stage in their lives, but the addiction.

Let me point out this truism, when a person is addicted, the only thing that matters is obtaining and using their agent of choice - that's it! You are wondering why they will not tithe, come to Bible study regularly, attend Sunday school and worship consistently? Chemical dependency robs its victim of energy, motivation, character, integrity and the ability to commit to anything. Once a person is actively engaged in using substances, he or she has little desire to do much more. Non-participatory members is exactly what the Devil wants to happen in church. This group of church-goers pose no threat to his strategic plan to destroy God's houses before the return of our Lord and Savior Jesus Christ.

Many in the pews are indeed part-time lovers of God. Over the time of my Christian life, I have noticed that there are three types of believers:

1) Those who believe and attend worship because it appears to be politically correct to do so;

2) Those who attend for the show and need something or someone to talk about around the water cooler on Monday morning; and,

3) Those who attend because beyond a shadow of a doubt, they know, that they know, that they know, God is real in their hearts and souls.

Furthermore, for those of you who have found yourselves spiritually stuck in a double-minded lifestyle filled with acts of backsliding to support your addiction, behind the scenes activities such as petty crimes and drug dealing are short lived. Engaging in these activities will bring the addicted believer to an end through jail, institution, or death. The decision to continue down paths laid out by Satan will only produce added problems such as loss of family, jobs, income, dignity, spirituality and hope, all of which are the associated behaviors of addiction. However, do not give up!

I would like to inform you that God is a redeeming God and a present help in a time of need. One significant fact is that He is available to us all. You too can be released from a journey towards an ultimate end of Hell and damnation caused by drug abuse and alcoholism. You can accomplish such by trusting God and reuniting your spirit with the Lord Jesus. Learn to abide in Him and He promises to abide in and with you. All you have to do is surrender to God in order to win the battle.

We must omit any opportunity to be used by the adversary and we must understand that our secrets are our sicknesses. Easier said than done, I'm certain. It is hard to conceptualize being saved, sanctified and sloppy drunk every day of our lives except on Sunday (morning)! It may be alarming to calculate how many believers in the pews on Sunday mornings are in spiritual bondage. While the pastor is in the middle of the morning message, these in bondage are thinking about how much they need to withhold from their tithes and offering to ensure the likelihood of being able to get stoned right after they leave church.

You may be surprised how many cars in the parking lots of urban churches have in their possession, stashes of substances that are cocked, rocked and ready to roll just as soon as the believer is out of the vision path of other recognizable members. This double-mindedness will only aid in a fallen belief system of generations that will follow. The same will ultimately affect the offspring of the church as well.

Substance abuse in any community presents maladaptive patterns of behavior. Addicted believers suffer with negative self-concepts. The conflict with self and God both produce damaging cultural ideologies among the people of faith around the globe.

THE VOICE OF ONE CRYING OUT IN THE WILDERNESS

Many weekly church-going, Bible-toting Christians have generationally engaged in years of involvement with alcohol and substance-abusing associates outside the wall of the parish. I have seen church leaders stopping in local service stations prior to arriving to church purchasing lottery tickets with God's finances and arriving to church to teach Sunday school lessons.

The Devil's spirit of addiction does not discriminate from country to country, state to state, city to city, community to community, church to church, pew to pew, position to position, family to family, or person to person. He (the adversary) intends to wipe out the army of God. Once again, his motive is to kill, steal and destroy. To win any war, one must have a strategic plan and adequate armaments. As his plan of attack, the Devil uses the spirit of addiction to slow down the believer. Make no mistake about it, he and his imps possess the weapons to destroy the opponent, if allowed.

Using substances blinds us from our true anointing and purpose in God. Addiction assures the Devil of the reality that this subculture of believers has developed a primary focus on their substance of choice and a secondary focus of serving God. One of the key elements in warfare is to catch your opponent by surprise and overtake them before they realize you are there. Addiction does exactly that; its claim to fame is to sneak up on its victims, and render mass destruction against its unsuspecting target. The weapons of mass destruction come in many forms. The Devil's intent is to destroy the body of Christ by using any means necessary.

LET US COUNT THE COST

The magnitude of stress and anguish caused by the spirit of addiction has no real measurable boundary. There are no limits to the devastation it can and will cause the addicted believer. The spirit can and will stretch from the house of the addicted believer and afflict the Lord's house. Often, family members attend weekly church services masking the pain caused by the dysfunctional environment in which they live day in and day out. It is not unusual to see a grandmother, a mother or even a wife crying throughout the morning worship service with the hope for change in their heart, while at the same time praying and petitioning God for help with family concerns.

Whether we accept it or not, addiction IS a family problem and these families need help! When this spirit enters a home it can only produce destruction. This destruction can come in many forms but be certain, it will come sooner or later if deliverance is not sought after by the addicted believer.

Denial is the greatest strategy used by Satan when afflicting addiction on church members and the surrounding community. The following are just a few areas affected by the consequences birthed out of addiction:

Socially: Through social embarrassment and shame, church attendance drops by the user and his or her family. Isolation becomes a way of life for family members due to guilt and shame. Members of the family become products of the addiction. This leads them to become children of addiction and adult children of addiction, all of which impacts their ability to socialize and grow into healthy people of God.

Psychologically: When addicts tell family members lies, too many times, family members find themselves furiously searching for evidence to support their suspicions. Often, over the years these untruths can cause family members to develop unresolved trust issues. In many cases, because of the indwelling trust issues and their disturbing upbringing, this same population cannot find a way to even trust God.

Emotionally: Living with an addicted believer is like being on an amusement park ride minus the fun aspect. The ups and downs and the around and around of emotional mood swings become quite dizzying. The emotions of anger, frustration, confusion, despair, hopelessness, guilt and shame can and often does paralyze one emotionally for life if allowed to continue.

Physically: The stress of living in a chronic state of chaos and being on edge all the time can wear anyone down, let alone an entire family. This chaos often leads to other physical illnesses with family members and can include anxiety, depression, headaches, migraines, digestive disorders, hypertension, diabetes and heart problems. Not to omit mental health, there are ongoing concerns for the user as well as for the users' family members touched by the dark spirit, such as suicidal and homicidal ideations.

Financially: Remember the 50 homes discussed earlier relative to usage of substances in the local churches' surrounding community? Now, let's examine the possible economic factors that involved in pathological community use.

Let's assume for the sake of our conversation that one person in each household is afflicted by the spirit of addiction and that $25.00 per day is spent purchasing substances. Based on that assumption, I have put together the following chart that illustrates addiction's devastating financial impact on one to 1000 households (which of course impacts the community and the church) over a 20-year span.

1 Person 1 House	1 Day $25.00	1 Year $9,125	10 Years $91,250	20 Years $182,500
50 Persons 50 Houses	1 Day $1,250	1 Year $456,250	10 Years $4,562,500	20 Years $9,125,000
100 Persons 100 Houses	1 Day $2,500	1 Year $912,500	10 Years $9,125,000	20 Years $18,250,000
1000 Persons 1000 Houses	1 Day $25,000	1 Year $9,125,000	10 Years $91,250,000	20 Years $182,500,000

Now we can better understand their resistance to "bring all the tithe into the store house…" (Malachi 3:8-10 KJV). After getting their weekly fix, there is nothing left for tithes, especially when the addicted believers are more often than not, living on fixed incomes. This should be a life-changing cost factor. Yet, many within the community become defensive when the local church asks for an offering to aid the church's mission work within the community. The spirit of addiction blinds its users to the godly image in which they were created, keeping the users fumbling in the dark to just get by, and, thereby holding captive the users' greatness.

CHAPTER FOUR
YOU ARE NOT ALONE

The Lord shall fight for you, and ye shall hold your peace.

Exodus 14:14

Every Sunday, massive numbers of Christians assemble in local churches, temples, and mega worship centers to proclaim their belief in the Gospel of Jesus Christ. Wearing their Sunday best, they gather to give their praises to the Almighty God. The choirs are singing, the praise dancers are dancing and the deacons are militarily positioned with the finance committee close by. The ushers are in control of the floor and the stage is set for the speaker of the hour.

The pulpit is filled with the anointed presence of the pastor and his or her associates. The parishioners are garbed in their St. John, Steve Harvey and Ralph Lauren Polo designer apparel and the floor is filled with enough colored reptiles to start a zoo. Both men and women parishioners can be seen donning alligator, crocodile, and snakeskin shoes, belts, and handbags. The sight of the assembly's attire alone would lead you to believe that to be saved guarantees you the opportunity to become prosperous and financially secure, or, minimally, to dress very nice!

When one arrives at the local church, he or she enters into an atmosphere of obvious external celebration; you would think that they have arrived at the eternal gates of Heaven right here on earth. The sight of the presentation alone brings one to tears of joy. The music stimulates the masses and the church is swaying from side-to-side with the fire of praise and worship.

The choir director appears to have the control of a seasoned Detroit Symphony Orchestra leader. The anointed movement of hand gestures stirs up the gifts and talents of the tenor, alto, soprano and bass sections of the praise and worship team. The organist, keyboardist, drummer and rhythm section are unified in every sense as the harmonic sound ripples throughout the sanctuary. There is not a dry eye in the place. Tears of adoration fill every eye in the room as songs to Zion are sent forth from the mouths of the saints in acts of humble temporal submission to God. The Mother's Board is positioned in a unified stance against the wiles of the Devil, with their systematic tapping of feet and clapping of hands. The music ministry is at its highest moment.

Arriving into the midst of the edifice, one could only assume that they have entered into the presence of angels. "Glory to God" and "Hallelujah is the highest praise," are shouted from the congregational pews. The church leadership can barely contain their purposefully still poses because of the heaviness of the anointed praise. This is the day to give God the glory and honor He deserves. It is Sunday and it is a new day full of new promises and new possibilities. This is the day that the Lord has made. Let us rejoice and be glad in it!

This presentation is what we encounter weekly as we enter into our various worship communities. It may be the norm, but there are some Christians who have mastered the art of masking their inner pain, emotional despairs, fears and suffering during the two to three hours of Sunday worship experience. Sunday after Sunday the houses of prayer are filled with zealous parishioners seeking answers from the pulpit. Many worshippers come from homes that are often saturated and consumed with undisclosed pain resulting from various forms of substance abuse. Believe it or not, our churches have the biggest cast of non-professional actors in the world. Hollywood would never have a cast shortage if executives would stop by the local church on any given Sunday.

Many of our parishioners seem to have become content with hiding behind the shadows of their abuse or the truth about their shortcomings, character flaws, and hidden iniquities. Denying a need for counseling to treat their pathological drinking and undisclosed substance abuse seems to be the norm when addiction is in control. The problem is that many addicted believers continue down the path of spiritual deception, which ultimately causes harm in the faith community as well as in their need to have a closer walk with God. Those who do seek help often go to other pastors and other churches in order to keep their addiction from being discovered by their own personal pastor or others within their local faith community. One great thing, however, is that these at least seek out solutions to their backslidden state.

Let me be clear, I am in no way saying that the entire body of Christ is full of people who are addicted. The church is the Bride of Christ, thus anything connected to Our Lord and Savior is Holy! I am, however, addressing the brokenness within the souls of the people in the body of Christ. I trust, support and wholeheartedly believe in the need to gather together as a family of believers.

There are broken spirits within the lives of many in congregations around the globe. I am simply pointing out what others may want to say, but have not been given the assignment to do so. God chooses whosoever He wants to carry His message.

After being delivered myself from this addicted spirit, God has chosen me in this season, to testify and to assure other believers that God understands your condition and your fears. I have been charged by God to inform the addicted believer that He is a very present help in times of need. He is no respecter of persons. We as believers are called to stand on the certainty that God will help us get through the roughest parts of our life's journey.

You may have found yourself uttering the words "Lord, why have thou forsaken me?" Have you ever felt that life was just not working for you? Have you ever uttered these words, "I thought that once I became a born-again believer, a child of God, my life would reflect my beliefs? I thought that my crown was able to lighten the load of my cross!" Well, you are not alone! Welcome to the world of ministry.

The Devil wants the believer to be filled with not just the spirit of addiction, but also with the spirit of doubt and the spirit of failure as well. It is his goal, and again, the war strategy that he uses. These and many other mental attacks may continue to haunt the addicted day in and day out if the Devil has his way. More often than not, many Christians have, at some point in their walk with God, admitted to having been right where you are.

Being a Christian is not without struggles and challenges; we are all subject to them both. God promises that He will be there with us each step of the way. When we understand our anointing in Christ Jesus, we will often understand the need to become fully equipped with the "full armor of God." God's armor helps lead us to serve God more effectively and fight the Devil and his imps more boldly. The Lord wants us to be close to Him in every way imaginable.

THE SPIRIT OF ADDICTION IS A STRATEGY OF WAR

For the sake of repetition, this warfare affects its human victims with a spiritual assault on their body, mind, and soul. The nature of addiction is like the characteristics of the adversary, the Devil, the father of all lies, who roams like a roaring lion seeking someone to devour. Once the Devil can alter the mind of the believer, he takes control through his use of dark spiritual forces. What are these spiritual forces that have continued to launch missiles of despair, depression and anxiety with such a staggering affect when they make contact with the chosen of God? How has the spirit of addiction managed to enter holy places?

When examining the fallout within the ranks of the local church congregations resulting from these assaults, we clearly discover casualties of war throughout the pews. However, as with any battleground aftermath, it is important to maintain hope and seek out the possibility that there are survivors.

When we carefully look at the impact that the spirit of addiction has caused the church, we may be excited to discover battle-weary believers who have desperately held on to their faith in Christianity over the years. Their armament of faith, though torn and shattered, has managed to save them from devastating blows of the Devil's assault. Because Satan is the subtle beast of the earth and his practices are designed to offend God, he uses tools such as addiction to overtake the believer. Consequently, he uses mechanisms which resemble himself.

The spirit of addiction is so subtle, cunning, baffling and fatal, that many long-term, unapologetic believers and dogmatic church attendees are now finding themselves teetering on the edge of backsliding. The devices used to promote their falling off are entrenched in lifestyles easily penetrated by acts of addiction. Social pressures and unresolved issues with righteousness seem to have triggered a black-out in their relationship with God. This loss of spiritual consciousness in the relationship between the believer and God is what Satan hopes for and remember, it's his ultimate goal. So when fighting a war, sometimes innocent people are hurt. Casualties of war happen every day in combat. This is to say, the enemy- the Devil, attacks saints, seasoned and unseasoned alike.

Addiction robs one of energy, motivation, character, integrity and the ability to commit to anything. As I stated previously, once the user is actively engaged in the addiction process he or she has little desire to do much more than that.

This is exactly what the Devil wants. He thrives on recruiting non-participatory members into his realm. This group of church-goers is no threat to his strategic plan to destroy the houses of God, but they are a part of the plan. Once these bench warmers are in his control, the idea of addiction almost seems acceptable within the body of Christ. He can now move on to the next phase of his strategy: infiltrating the minds of more seasoned saints. If he is successful in his attack, some, knowing the way, start wearing masks in the hope of hiding and distinguishing themselves from bench warmers.

Trapped within every Christian is the hope to be more connected to God. The most important quality of our walk with God is our relationship with our Creator. We were created to please God with our service to Him and through service we are given the ability to commune with

Him. Changes in lifestyle happen when we are willing to establish the discipline to walk a walk of faith. If you want to lie at His feet, commune with Him and create such a relationship with the Lord each day. Discipline and faith are key.

The truth is not always comfortable, especially for those of you who have found yourselves caught up in a double-minded lifestyle of Sunday morning worship followed by weekly activities to support your addiction. I would like to remind you again that God is a redeeming God, and a very present help in your time of need. The most significant fact is that He is available to us all. You too can be released from a journey charged with drug abuse and alcoholism where the ultimate end is hell and damnation. The battle is already won, if you believe!

DITCH YOUR MASK OF DENIAL AND DECEPTION

Just as many of you will have to do as a means to reconnect with God on a sincere level, I had to feel my way out of the demonic mess I had made of my life. I had to surrender and I had to ask the Holy Spirit to lead me to a place where I had the opportunity to escape.

As a previous victim of these same spiritual attacks brought on by the spirit of addiction, I was blinded on every side of my walk with God. You see, I loved the Lord but I loved my substances as well. I faithfully attended church, sang in the choir and worked on the usher board for years. Just like many of you, I thought my addiction was hidden from my fellow saints.

I did not have money to support the mission of the church because the only mission I was on at the time was feeding my addicted spirit. As a result, much of my life at that time was in isolation and segregation. I did not feel connected to anything or anyone. I did not fit in with the church or even with the un-churched, which kept me alone most of the time.

As a result of being led by the addiction spirit instead of the Holy Spirit, I had gotten on the wrong ramp of life. I was traveling down a road whose endings were ultimately bottomless pits of despair, denial, destruction and spiritual bankruptcy.

There are too many believers who are still suffering behind a mask of spiritual contentment with addiction shadows under the pews of the local urban churches. Paralyzed with deceit and full of the pain that comes from being in spiritual bankruptcy, this population of believers continue the spiritual smoke screen of Sunday morning worship, Wednesday night Bible study, and Friday evening prayer services. Living inside mental containers lined with the substances of choice, inner walls of the addicted are filled with pictures of lies and distorted realities of what it means to be a believer of the Most High God while still practicing the art of addiction. They continue their perpetration of happiness despite wearing undergarments soiled in total despair, camouflaged underneath a mask that hides their sickness.

Many live daily with pain and hurt because of an inability to end compulsive behaviors. Such are designed to destroy their hope and relationship with the ultimate power source, the Almighty God. These often attend church service until the guilt and shame of addiction forces withdrawal into isolation, segregation and denial of the power within. This ultimately causes many believers to run from the gospel and eventually fall away from fellowship with other Christians.

I want to be honest about what I have been through in my years of serving the Lord. As a pastor, I was once perplexed about the lack of retention in the church I served and oftentimes I felt a sense of inadequacy. However, the Lord God revealed to me one night during my prayer time that there has been an infiltration of spiritual assaults against the body of Christ (the church), a spiritual disease planted by the Devil. As with any onslaught on the cells in the body, once an infection develops, there is a need to administer an antibiotic.

God Almighty has revealed to me that through the sharing of issues inspired by this reading, we will be able to administer that antibiotic for those who are seeking relief and an opportunity for a renewed relationship with the Creator. It is the spiritual antibiotic needed to cure the spiritual infection that has developed within the walls of the local church, a virus that if not contained, will continue to spread across the world in epidemic proportions.

Trust issues are a major concern for people afflicted with chemical dependency. It is hard for believers who are chemically dependent to come out of the closet.

IF HE DID IT BEFORE HE CAN DO IT AGAIN

I too have had my fill of storms prior to my deliverance from the spirit of addiction. Of course, as with any severe storm, there are damages and often some degree of loss. For me, these losses would include family, friends, physical and mental health. In some moments of my addiction journey, I felt the loss of my own spirituality and connection with God.

When reflecting on past events of my life, I recall feeling a significant detachment from communication with God. I went to church, but sat in the back of the balcony out of shame and guilt. I wanted to fit in and migrate into the congregation's anointing, but the substances made me feel inadequate and dirty.

God does have a way of using even the filth that comes with our sin and the spirit of addiction for His glory. I recognized that I needed to grow spiritually to share my personal testimony and perspectives with the world on living in the urban areas of the city of Detroit. God gave me this perspective after getting delivered from years of a painful struggle trying to survive. I struggled with surviving in a culture and community that afforded me, and many like me, - without any confrontation, - the opportunity to continue the destructive path of addiction.

Being a servant for the Lord is hard, and quite frankly impossible, when you are living a double life. We are unable to serve two masters. Once I was able to assess and admit that the abnormal behavior that I thought was normal had to cease, it then became evident to me that I needed deliverance. Early in the process of my deliverance I began to discover that my compulsive and obsessive behavior had led me to the point of surrendering my anointing over to the Devil. I had dropped down my weaponry and ultimately put my faith and relationship with God on hold.

This very act of submission to the Devil's spirit of addiction and to the wiles of his assigned imps on my life, led me to a season filled with moments of spiritual defeat. He attacked the core of my integrity and my spiritual manhood by using the spirit of addiction and other maladaptive and maladjusted ideologies on life. The spirit of addiction caused me to destroy my home and later turned my youthful ambitions into hopeless scenes of despair.

Alcohol and drugs turned me into a brute and a derelict. If the anti-social behavior associated with my addiction was not enough of a problem on its own, then the perpetuation of my petty criminal behavior certainly added to my world of destructive, compulsive and obsessive activities. My desire to serve God did not leave me but my substance use deactivated it. My hope in life was disjointed and my dreams became disoriented nightmares. I was indeed a hot mess. I walked like an agnostic, talked like an atheist and looked like a demon from the pit of hell.

I allowed the Devil and his assigned imps to put my life on demonic auto-pilot. I was on a trip with no destination; I was a dead man walking. I was in my own secret storm, searching for tomorrow, on the edge of night, being young and restless, as the world turned, seeking out destruction throughout the days of my life, with a need to be admitted into the general hospital.

With lost hope, cloudy vision and a missing relationship with God, I was like the fishermen on the lake washing their nets when Jesus showed up. Like these men, I too was ready to quit, ready to throw in the towel and pull in the net of life. I was so far into substance use and like many in this captive state, I felt defeated with just the thought of life, family, employment and God.

Sometimes the thought would enter my mind, "Would God Almighty accept me and embrace me just as I am? Could God make a difference in my life after so many years of substance use?" These were inquiries that filled my thoughts each morning I was forced to wake up.

What saddens my heart is that far too many citizens of Zion are rendered defenseless when seen engaging in substance use or abuse with both Bible and bottle in hand. Unfortunately, too many addicted believers are attending Bible study, prayer meetings, and choir rehearsal even after consuming their substance of choice. They are consumed with the hope that the smell of substance will not alert anyone in the area. These and other significant signs are recent indicators that there is simply too much denial among many who enter the house of prayer.

The irony is that the power to change is right within their reach; yet the Devil's influence subdues those efforts. The addicted fail to accept that God through Jesus Christ is their power source, a power which specializes in tearing down strongholds. However, in order to begin to seek ways and means to find your way out of hell, you must first believe that you are truly in hell. One must accept that the only person being fooled is oneself.

I understand that it is not easy to begin discussion about the "isms" in our lives, but it is necessary if we are going to be used by God. We must eliminate any opportunity to be used by the adversary and we must understand that our secrets are our sicknesses. Easier said than done, I'm certain. It is hard to conceptualize being saved, sanctified, and sloppy drunk every day of our lives, except on Sunday.

CHAPTER FIVE

THERE IS NO PLACE LIKE HOME

For everything, absolutely everything above and below, visible and invisible, everything got started in him and finds its purpose in him.

Colossians 1:16 (MSG)

In this final chapter I will give three principles that will assist you in your deliverance, your restoration and hopefully your ultimate return back home to God the Father. Use of these principles were paramount in my personal deliverance in 1986. Since then, the daily use of these spiritual nuggets has increased my ability to hear from God in a most sustainable way. Addiction take us so far away from what God originally intended for our lives here on earth, that it becomes hard sometimes to think He still cares. Getting back on track with our spirituality is essential for survival and for the deliverance process to take place. God is our Creator and He can fix anything broken in our life.

When we have been out of fellowship for so long due to addiction, we lose something within our relationship with God and other believers. Sometimes this loss has little to do with our church attendance, but it has everything to do with the mental and emotional state of being at church, while not being in church! The addictive believers' spiritual momentum slows down because of the nature and purpose of the attack. Hopefully, one will discover that addiction has left us spiritually void.

If you are addicted or know someone addicted, please realize the urgency to seek help that will assist in three areas:

1) your deliverance;

2) relinquishing the double-mindedness that accompanies addiction, and

3) your return to spiritual activities centering on church and Christian fellowship.

The longer we are out of fellowship with God, or the longer we stay away from His presence, the harder it becomes to return.

In the gospel of Luke there is a significant passage, which is in my opinion, the greatest example of the need for deliverance from the demonic spirit used against unsuspecting saints:

> *Then the younger son gathered up all that was his and traveled far away to another country. There he wasted his money in foolish living. When he realized what he was doing, he thought, all of my father's servants have plenty of food. But I am here, almost dying with hunger. I will leave and return to my father and say to him, father, I have sinned against God and have done wrong to you. So the son left and went home to his father. So the son left and went to his father. While the son was still a long way off, his father saw him and felt sorry for his son. So the father ran to hug him and kissed him. The son said I have sinned against God and have done you wrong. I am no longer worthy to be called your son. But the father said to his servant to prepare for a party because his son which once was dead, but is now alive again. He was lost but is now found, so they began to celebrate.*
> Luke 15:13-24 (NCV)

Believers are here on earth to put a smile on God's face! Satan knows that the purpose of your life is far greater than your own personal understanding or need for fulfillment. The Devil purposed to be successful with stealing believers' hopes and dreams via addiction's vicious attack.

But remember, the Devil is a liar, and you can be victorious over his attack on your mind.

He has told you that you are all alone in the fight for your life, and that too is a lie from the pit of which he has climbed out. God has a plan for you and He is working it out for your good. Your struggle with this particular spirit is all for a purpose. When you come out of this you will be able to sing praises to God.

God often sends us through things to bring us to things. He allows us to go through struggles so we may be able to have a reason to praise Him when we come out on the other side victorious. Our lives are living testimonies so that God can get the glory out of our story.

In the story of Joseph, he was sold off by his own brothers for a few coins because of their envy and jealous attitude toward him. Joseph was chosen early by God for a special season, which was to come later in his life. He went into slavery in a most unfortunate way. The story unfolds with tragedy and ends in triumph.

As Joseph moved from the pit to the prison to the palace, God's hand was constantly upon him.

He reunited with his hard-hearted brothers later in the story. He shared with them that what was meant for evil,

God used it for His good! God knows all about you and He has a plan for your life bigger than you can imagine. Just trust Him and He will see you through because He cannot and will not lie.

Joseph, however, had a pride problem. Pride can often cause blindness in our hearts. Pride is said to come before the fall, which brings me to my first principle.

Principle # 1 - ACCEPTANCE

> *I know that nothing good lives in me, that is, in my sinful nature. For I have the desire to do what is good, but I cannot carry it out.*
> *Romans 7:18 (NIV)*

THE SIN SOLUTION

Sin, in any form, robs us of our inheritance in Jesus. It attacks our serenity, and it deactivates our Christian value system. When the spirit of addiction is active, it is like a runaway train, speeding through the user's mind. However, there is a solution to ending the destructive process of sin and addiction. The process begins with acceptance of your state and becoming aware of the need to REPENT and to reignite your spiritual life.

The addicted believer or non-believing addict must both come to a point of acceptance that all are powerless over sin. Because of your acts of sin, you have become separated from your relationship with God the Father. This is vitally important to the initial stage of surrendering your will, because again, spirituality is extremely important in the deliverance process. God is a spirit and we must approach Him in spirit. Remember our weapons are not carnal, but are in fact spiritual.

This spiritual revival is needed because the spirit of addiction can become so powerful that it competes with the spiritual power given to us by God. I want to reacquaint you with the awareness that when using substances, the associated lifestyles usually replace the space once held by your spiritual activities. Rediscovering your life with God will help restore order in your life and reconnect you with the Holy Spirit. This reconnection will assist you in putting your addiction in perspective. Walking with the Father allows you the possibility to regain your focus and remind you that you have more power than the spirit of addiction has over your life. This principle encourages one to understand that we can do nothing without the power of God. And with His power spiritual transformation is obtainable.

CHRISTIAN VALUES

When we examine our spirituality and discover how far we have fallen away from our walk with God, we can clearly see how we have allowed Satan's demonic spirits to rob us of our morality and integrity. Christian values play a critical role in our deliverance from the spirit of addiction. These values are one of the most significant keys to escape the spirit of addiction's locks.

When we examine our Christian values, we often attribute them to what we learned in the Word of God. These values are your beliefs that things are right and good, that other things are wrong and bad, and that somethings are more important than others. They help us understand that one way of doing something is better than another.

Christian values are usually deeply held – originating from your earliest learning and background, reflecting what your parents taught you, what you learned in school and religious institutions, and what social and cultural influences are held as right and wrong. These deeply held learnings are stolen from the believer once they return to the worldly system of living without Christ. However, God will restore, replace, and return all that has been stolen from you once you repent and return to Him.

> *And I will restore to you the years that the locust hath eaten, the canker worm, and the caterpillar, and then palmerworm, my great army which I sent among you.*
>
> Joel:2:25 (KJV)

RESTORING THE RELATIONSHIPS WITH GOD

God is waiting to restore you to your rightful position in His Kingdom. Life presents challenges daily, and if not careful, these events can put a rip in our relationship with God. We must move quickly toward repairing those areas that have fallen apart. Love for God lasts forever. God wants you to be in close fellowship with Him and other Christians to get the true benefit of your deliverance. Our values are not luxuries rather they are necessities in our lives.

A frighteningly common way that we repeat yesterday is by continuing to do what we already know doesn't work. People who repeat yesterday are in motion with no direction. The spirit of addiction is like pedaling hard on a stationary bike. You may see result on the screen but in reality, you are going nowhere. Restoring your Christian values will produce measurable growth and sustainable rewards.

Principle # 2- SURRENDER

> *My grace is sufficient for you, for my power is made perfect in weakness.*
>
> *2 Corinthians 12:9 (NIV)*

The spirit of addiction must yield to the authority of Jesus.

You must come to understand the benefit of grace and how it operates in the lives of believers. Through the Father, the Son and the Holy Spirit, you can be restored to your rightful positon in the Kingdom of God. Your faith must lead you to the certainty that restoration of your mind, body, and spirit is within your reach. Know that God wants to celebrate your return home, not just as a servant but as His child, and heir to the benefit of a renewed relationship with the Trinity.

The fact remains that if it is possible for believers to give ground to the enemy, then it is possible, in fact it is crucial, for believers under the power of the Holy Spirit, to take back the ground that was surrendered to the enemy. When it comes to spiritual warfare and spiritual victory we must remember that we are not in a battle against "flesh and blood," but spiritual darkness and evil forces.

We must resist the Devil on all fronts: in our minds, in our bodies, and in our spirits. Actively resisting the Devil, and acknowledging your need for grace in the situation of addiction will ignite your release from the grips of the enemy.

Rededicate your body to glorifying God. Study the Word daily as you draw near to God. Fix your thoughts and actions on the things of Christ Jesus. All this will aid you in cleansing your hands of inequity, your heart of deceit, and your mind of binary. God will do the rest!

> *Study to shew thyself approved unto God, a workman that needth not to be ashamed, rightly dividing the word of truth.*
> 2 Timothy 2:15 (KJV)

Beyond a shadow of a doubt, Bible reading is a must to aid in self-cleansing. Studying the scripture supplies the believer with current strategies that assures the believer defeat over the deceiver.

Even Satan knows that God is not simply a concept or a doctrine. He is a Person who seeks a close, one-on-one relationship with you and me. God does not want us to merely believe in Him, He wants to relate to us on a personal level. He does not just want to hear us recite prayers. He wants to converse with us. God's plan is not to abandon Christians once we are born again. God wants to play an active part in our daily life. Reading his Word allows God the opportunity to speak with His children daily. When we search the scriptures, we can discover the meaning and direction God has for our lives, and just as important we will be able to hear Him share with us the plan for our life with Him as our Father.

Often without question, the decisions we make are based on ideas we have already accepted. Wrong ideas lead to wrong conclusions. In the past when the spirt of addiction would show up, we followed any and everything it forced us to do.

The truth is as believers of God we leave our first love when we lose our daily awareness of our need for God's presence in our lives. When we return to reading the Word of God we in fact begin a new relationship with our love, a new awareness and a new desire to be like Jesus.

Since the Bible is God's Word, studying it is a way to know God better. Through His words, we come to know not only the nature and attributes of God, but we also come to understand His plan for each of us. In a greater sense, we also come to know God's plan in history, His sovereignty, His providence, His love and more. Without studying the Word of God, there is only so much we can learn. But with it we can know God better because the Bible is God's Word to us and Jesus is the Word made flesh.

> *That He might sanctify and cleanse it with the washing of water by the word.*
> *Ephesians 5:26 (KJV)*

Principle #3- DISCIPLINE

Encourage yourself by fasting and praying in the Spirit for continued deliverance.

"He said to them, 'this kind cannot come out except by prayer and fasting'" (Mark 9:29).

Take control of your thoughts by:

Casting down imaginations and every high thing that exalts itself against the knowledge of God, bringing every thought into captivity to the obedience of Christ.
2 Corinthians 10:5 (KJV)

Fasting and Prayer are the best antidotes to our confused thinking. It can and will cancel the agenda of the Devil every time. Fasting and prayer is voluntarily going without food in order to focus on prayer and fellowship with God. Fasting and prayer often go hand in hand, but this is not always the case. You can pray without fasting, and fast without prayer. It is when these two events are combined and devoted to God's glory that they reach their full effectiveness. Having a dedicated time of prayer and fasting is not a way of manipulating God into doing what you desire. Rather, it is simply forcing yourself to focus and rely on God for the strength, provision, and wisdom you need. Deliverance from the spirit of addiction takes work! Not superficial work, but real work, the type of work that will announce to the Devil you are serious about becoming an overcomer.

THE WARFARE OF FASTING

But you, beloved, build yourselves up in your most holy faith. Praying in the Holy Spirit.
                                    Jude 1:20 (KJV)

The Bible gives numerous accounts of fasting and prayer. Occasions and circumstances often called for fasting, individually as well as community fasting. As outlined in allaboutbible.com, the Old Testament law specifically requires prayer and fasting for the Day of Atonement. The custom itself later became known as "the day of fasting" (Jeremiah 36:6) or "the Fast" (Acts 27:9). The following are examples of when fasting and prayer produced the sought after result for those who petitioned God for aid:

- Moses fasted during the 40 days and 40 nights that he was on Mount Sinai receiving the law from God (Exodus 34:28).

- David fasted when he learned that Saul and Jonathan had been killed (2 Samuel 1:12).

- Esther had the entire Jewish community fast with her for three days before approaching the king to request an intervention on behalf of her people's lives (Esther 3:16).

- Nehemiah had a time of prayer and fasting upon learning that Jerusalem was still in ruins (Nehemiah 1:4).

- Darius, the king of Persia, fasted all night after he was forced to put Daniel in the lions' den (Daniel 6:18).

All the weapons used by Satan to keep the believer from spending time with God, proves that he is threatened by the act of prayer and fasting. Keep your joy level strong.

> *Do not be grieved, for the joy of the Lord is your strength.*
> *Nehemiah 8:10 (KJV)*

Prayer and fasting also occurs in the New Testament.

- John the Baptist taught his disciples to fast (Mark 2:18).

- Jesus fasted for 40 days and 40 nights before His temptation by Satan (Matthew 4:2).

- The church of Antioch fasted (Acts 13:2) and sent Paul and Barnabas off on their first missionary journey (Acts 13:3).

- Paul and Barnabas spent time in prayer and fasting for the appointment of elders in the churches (Acts 14:23).

The Word of God does not specifically command believers to spend time in prayer and fasting. However, history indicates the act as being significant in seeking God for results. At the same time, prayer and fasting is definitely something we should be undertaking. And if deliverance from the spirit of addiction is your goal, then you will need to become a prayer and fasting warrior.

> *For the flesh lusteth against the Spirit, and the Spirt against the flesh: and these are contrary the one to the other: so that ye cannot do the things that ye would.*
>
> *Galatian 5:17 (KJV)*

Remember, the focus of prayer and fasting is not just on abstaining from food. Christians should engage in fasting to take our eyes off the things of this world and focus our thoughts on God. Fasting becomes the referee between the Spirit and the flesh. By taking our eyes off the things of this world through prayer and biblical fasting, we can focus better on Christ. God is like a mirror. The mirror never changes, but everyone who looks into it sees something different.

THE WARFARE OF PRAYER

The battle against the Devil and his spirit of addiction is real. Your life depends on you winning. You must not forget you have an enemy that thrives on keeping you oppressed. Because prayer is a spiritual discipline, Satan attacks our mind and discourages us from praying as often as we should. He is extremely terrified when we fast and pray. All the weapons that the Devil uses against us to prevent us from praying or talking to God prove that he wants to alienate or separate us from God.

Prayer makes a way for God to act sovereignly on earth. Prayer that is based on faith bears fruit for the Kingdom and pleases God. When you pray, and communicate with God in faith, He will speak to you and give you direction, wisdom, knowledge, strength and protection. Deliverance from addiction begins with the deliverance of the mind first, and this can only happen through prayer and fasting! One final note on prayer is that remember God has a purpose for your life.

Regardless of the spiritual attack on your life by the spirit of addiction, your detour with substance use does not preclude the Almighty God from using you in His kingdom building agenda. Pray for guidance on the matter of your deliverance and He will grant you the wisdom needed to overcome the struggle to continue down the road of destruction with addiction. God is a promise keeper.

Now that you have embraced these three principles you are ready to return home just as the prodigal son returned. God is preparing a table for you in the presence of your enemy, Satan. Your cup will run over, and goodness and mercy shall follow all the days of your life. You can shine light on the darkness which has caused the shadow of addiction to fall on your pew life. Seize the moment and maximize the hour!

THE STORM IS PASSING OVER

> *To everything there is a season, and a time to every purpose under the heaven: A time to be born, and a time to die; a time to plant, and a time to pluck up that which is planted; A time to kill, and a time to heal; a time to break down, and a time to build up; A time to weep, and a time to laugh; a time to mourn, and a time to dance; A time to cast away stones, and a time to gather stones together; a time to embrace, and a time to refrain from embracing; A time to get, and a time to lose; a time to keep, and a time to cast away; A time to rend, and a time to sew; a time to keep silence, and a time to speak; A time to love, and a time to hate; a time of war, and a time of peace.*
> *Ecclesiastes 3:1-8 (KJV)*

Now as a delivered believer your season of redemption is upon you; take up your bed of affliction, rise and walk towards your victory. The time has now arrived where you can focus on the ultimate destiny in your life, your God promised opportunity to have the reward of eternal rest with our Lord Jesus Christ because of your decision to renew your relationship and your walk with God. The Father, the Son and the Holy Spirit are excited about your decision to repent, replenish, replace, recover, renew, revisit, and restore the image of God in you.

God has planted in you a fresh cry and a new direction which promotes a new commitment to life and your walk with Him. Now you will no longer be influenced to sway to the left or to the right by the wiles of the Devil for you now are spiritually equipped and aware. You see, your wrestle is not against flesh and blood, but against powers, and principalities, against the rulers of darkness of this world and against spiritual wickedness in high places.

Because you have chosen to shine your light of salvation on the Devil and his imps, you have afforded yourself the opportunity to clear out the shadows of addiction beneath your pew, I declare that victory is now yours. My Beloved, because you have sought the face of God today, the Lord God Almighty says to you:

> *"I have given you a new commitment, not houses, not land, not silver, not cash, not even crowds, or crowns. It is in fact the reward for your surrender to My will and*

My way of life. Because you have not retreated back to the spirit of your addiction, I have put you directly in the path of My righteousness, a righteousness that I have saved for you these years of separation from Me.

Time and seasons are no longer your enemies, but have become assets to your travels towards the destiny I have awaiting you, as it is for all those who call upon My name; they shall be saved. You must remember that you are and have always been a King of kings kid with a Kingdom agenda stitched inside the inner wall of your heart, and because of your relational connection to Me, the Father, no weapons formed against you shall prosper.

You will be able to discern and be able to distinguish for sure throughout this new season of your life that you are truly reborn again, and you are now for the first time in your walk with Your Lord and Your God, living in a new place. Your prayers for deliverance during the midnights of your walking the streets of despair, seeking solutions to the cravings of the spirit of addiction have not gone unheard. Your break-of-day moans and tears of 'here I go again' have not gone unfelt. I watched with compassion and patience as you have worshipped Me, and have called for Me in the midst of your pain and suffering. Each moment of your despair, I dispatched angels to you each time you sent for Me; through your brokenness you have summoned Me into your presence, and because of your faith and belief in My Word, you are now delivered.

Because of the authority and power I possess and give unto you this day, you are positioned in a place you have never been, you are standing in a place in My presence that I have never opened to you before, a place that I have never unfolded to you, a place that I have never revealed to you and that existed; but because you have turned your face to Me today, because you have turned your heart and you have said out of your mouth, 'yes, I will seek His face and yes, I will turn from my wicked ways, and yes I will lay hold on Him,' I have heard you and in response, I have not given you wealth to calculate, but I have given you a new assurance.

This new relationship with Me will implant undisputable power against the enemy's attacks when activated through prayer and fasting, and through the power of my Word. What I have planted in you will not just last throughout this season of your life, but throughout your lifetime even until eternity. Because you have turned from your evil ways, I have put in you what you really need. I have put in you what is needed to turn from sin. And I have put in you what you need to turn from your own ambitions. I have put in you what is needed to turn from the world for the rest of your life," saith God.

IT'S TIME FOR A WARDROBE CHANGE

But in Mount Zion there shall be those who escape, and it shall be holy, and the house of Jacob shall possess their own possessions.
Obadiah 17 (ESV)

He rescued me from my strong enemy and from those who hated me, for they were too mighty for me.
Psalm 18:1 (ESV)

My final point to you my friends is that God has all power in His hand. This power is extended to the believer. Now that your pew has been cleansed from the shadow of addiction and despair, reach back and bring someone else to the place of surrender. We are our brother's keeper. The Almighty God saved us through His Son so we may teach others about the benefit of salvation through Christ Jesus, our Lord and Savior.

I AM AN OVERCOMER

For everyone who has been born of God overcomes the world. And this is the victory that has overcome the world our faith. Who is it that overcomes the world except the one who believes that Jesus is the Son of God.
1 John 5:1-5 (ESV)

May God richly bless your journey and may your deliverance become a testament of the goodness of God.

This is not the ending but the beginning…

ABOUT THE AUTHOR

Rev. Dr. Eural Alexander, Founder and Pastor
New Light Family Christian Center

Rev. Dr. Eural Alexander is an anointed, multi-gifted minister of the Gospel of Jesus Christ. He is a fearless champion of soul-winning for Christ with an uncompromising conviction, which causes demons to flee.

Dr. Alexander received his ministerial licensure and ordination at the Historic Little Rock Baptist Church in Detroit, Michigan. There, he was promoted to Associate Minister and served as Minister of Evangelism. He was called to pastor Beacon Light Missionary Baptist Church in April, 2000.

Ever obedient to God's instructions, Dr. Alexander founded New Light Family Christian Center in 2008. New Light is a family-focused Pentecostal, Bible-based teaching and preaching ministry. Through Holy Spirit's leading, the ministry empowers congregants with practical application of God's Word to affect purposeful, fruitful and impactful godly living.

Embracing 2 Timothy 2:15, Dr. Alexander is a scholar and learned man, having earned three of his five college degrees from the University of Detroit-Mercy. These include an Associate of Science in Counseling, a Bachelor of Science in Addiction Studies and a Master of Science in Counseling. Dr. Alexander also earned a Master of Arts in Pastoral Counseling from Marygrove College and a Doctor of Ministry in SpiritualFormation from Ecumenical Theological Seminary. With a heavy mantle to champion the marginalized, in 1986 Dr. Alexander founded CARE, INC. CARE is a State of Michigan licensed substance abuse and counseling agency, where he serves as Executive Director. Additionally, he is a Certified State of Michigan CAC-1 Addictions Counselor. CARE also functions as an outreach ministry of New Light, aiding in the healing and deliverance of those suffering with issues of substance abuse, gambling addiction, marital discord, and domestic violence.

Dr. Alexander has received numerous awards and accolades for his diverse community involvement and accomplishments. Dr. Alexander is most proud of The Ambassador of Peace Award, which was bestowed upon him for his missionary work in Israel. During his visit to the Holy Land, he was chosen from hundreds of clergy and given the esteemed honor of baptizing believers from all over the world in the River Jordan. Dr. Alexander gives all glory to God for such a blessed privilege.

In addition to being a faithful and mighty instrument of God, Dr. Alexander is a father and grandfather, as well as an awesome spiritual father to all of whom he under-shepherds. He is the loving and devoted husband of Dr. Beverly Alexander, an anointed and gifted ambassador of God, who supports his spiritual assignments, and, who ministers alongside him.

www.ingramcontent.com/pod-product-compliance
Lightning Source LLC
Chambersburg PA
CBHW020806160426
43192CB00006B/457